BRIGHT NOTES

THE EYE OF THE STORM AND OTHER WORKS BY PATRICK WHITE

Intelligent Education

Nashville, Tennessee

BRIGHT NOTES: The Eye of the Storm and Other Works
www.BrightNotes.com

No part of this publication may be used or reproduced in any manner whatsoever without written permission, except in the case of brief quotations in critical articles and reviews. For permissions, contact Influence Publishers http://www.influencepublishers.com.

ISBN: 978-1-645423-68-3 (Paperback)
ISBN: 978-1-645423-69-0 (eBook)

Published in accordance with the U.S. Copyright Office Orphan Works and Mass Digitization report of the register of copyrights, June 2015.

Originally published by Monarch Press.
Herbert Reaske, 1977
2020 Edition published by Influence Publishers.

Interior design by Lapiz Digital Services. Cover Design by Thinkpen Designs.

Printed in the United States of America.

Library of Congress Cataloging-in-Publication Data forthcoming.
Names: Intelligent Education
Title: BRIGHT NOTES: The Eye of the Storm and Other Works
Subject: STU004000 STUDY AIDS / Book Notes

CONTENTS

1)	Introduction to Patrick White	1
2)	Introduction to The Eye of the Storm	6
3)	Textual Analysis	9
	Chapter One	9
	Chapter Two	18
	Chapter Three	22
	Chapter Four	25
	Chapter Five	28
	Chapter Six	31
	Chapter Seven	35
	Chapter Eight	40
	Chapter Nine	48
	Chapter Ten	51
	Chapter Eleven	56
	Chapter Twelve	58
4)	Introduction to Voss	59
5)	Textual Analysis	65
	Voss: Chapters 1-5: Up to the Departure	65

	Voss: Chapters 6-13: The Approaches to Hell	73
	Voss: Chapters 14-16: The Afterglow	84
6)	The Aunt's Story	88
7)	The Tree of Man	93
8)	Riders in the Chariot	96
9)	The Solid Mandala	99
10)	The Vivisector	101
11)	Questions and Answers in Outline Form	104
12)	Bibliography	108

INTRODUCTION TO PATRICK WHITE

NOTE TO THE STUDENT

In this Critical Commentary, Professor Herbert Reaske aims to enhance your appreciation of the fiction of the great Australian writer, Patrick White. But Professor Reaske's discussion will make little sense to you unless you are already familiar with White's novels. Throughout his discussion, Professor Reaske assumes that it will prompt you to refer back continually to the original texts. In the United States, these are available in hardcover from Viking Press and in paperback from Avon Books.

—The Editors

PATRICK WHITE

Patrick White was awarded the Nobel Prize for Literature in 1973. His latest novel, *The Eye of the Storm,* had recently been published. Because of the high quality of the author's earlier books, it was widely and fully reviewed. There was much to praise but sometimes there were qualifications, particularly in Australia and America. The English were more enthusiastic. Even so *The Eye of the Storm* did not reach the best-seller lists until after the announcement. Suddenly the public wanted to know more about the author. Many had read perhaps one of his earlier books. What were the others? The second-hand book dealers were soon cleaned out. Who was Patrick White?

THE MAN

Many years ago White's grandfather had migrated to Australia. The family had become successful ranchers and property owners. They had money. When his father and mother were on a trip back to England in 1912, Patrick was born. He was still a baby when they returned to their native land. Patrick's childhood was spent there until he was thirteen when he was sent to England to be "ironed out." He has since said that the four years in the public school where he was enrolled were the most miserable of his life. In late adolescence he returned to Australia and became a "jackaroo" or ranch hand among the soft rolling hills behind the populated sea coast. At twenty he was a restless young man and made another trip to England. He read history at Cambridge and became expert in French and German. Afterwards he spent some time in London. He lived with literary people, painters, and actors. He wrote reviews and published a slim volume of poetry. By 1941 two novels had come out and were heralded as "promising."

World War II intervened. He became an intelligence officer assigned to the Middle East. The war left Europe, it seemed to him, physically and intellectually barren. Even London which was trying to make a comeback as a center for the arts was uninspiring. He travelled much on the continent, particularly in Germany. Once he went so far as to make a trip across the United States. Back in London he wrote *The Aunt's Story*, a novel that begins in Australia, climaxes in Europe, and ends in the United

States. It was published in England, Canada, and the United States, but not in Australia until many years later. At about this time White decided if he was to continue to develop as a novelist he must return to Australia. He was determined to write an all-Australian novel.

White went back to Sydney and has stayed there ever since except for brief trips abroad. With a friend he first bought a house some miles out of the city. They did some farming, raised dogs, and sold flowers. Meanwhile White continued to write and Sydney to expand until his homestead was fronted by a busy, traffic-grinding thoroughfare. Patrick White then packed his books and his paintings, many of his own and more that he had acquired in his effort to sponsor modern art in Australia. He moved back into town in a large Edwardian house, such as those for which Sydney is still famous. He likes the neighborhood and stays pretty much at home.

THE MAN'S ACHIEVEMENT

Because of his many novels there has become what is known as White's canon. In music a canon is a motif often repeated with variations; White has such a motif running through all his work. To simplify dangerously, it may be stated as the loneliness of all men in their attempts to communicate completely with others. In every man there is always something withheld or unrecognizable. Each of White's books contains at least one lonely person. In each book the variations are more important. Each **protagonist** appears in a different setting at different times. Sometimes we have a man, sometimes a woman, yet each is revealed in his relationship with others. It was because of this that the Nobel Prize Committee spoke of White's "**epic psychological art.**"

White's first novel written entirely in an Australian setting and written by him in Australia, *The Tree of Man*, misfired with his compatriots. Insofar as it dealt with the opening up of the land, it was in the tradition of current or even earlier Australian fiction. A seemingly ordinary young couple move out of a town and settle, with much hard work, on a home of their own. But they turn out not to be so ordinary. On the other hand their children grow up to be quite ordinary and far from exemplary. Australians were not pleased with White's picture of themselves.

The novels that seemed to satisfy them were usually of a journalistic type of **realism** stressing the virile pioneer, sometimes an ex-convict sent out from England, who struggled with the bush and the aboriginal bushmen. For all their **realism**, both whites and blacks were romanticized. The books were frequently historical in the Sir Walter Scott sense. The past was to shed light on the present.

White's perspective on modern life differs in several fundamental elements from that of most contemporary novelists. He is conscious of changes in culture that are submerged by affluence and its fantasies. The confidence of society in itself, brought about by science and industrialization, is with White secondary to the lack of confidence, mainly self-confidence, to be found in individual men. Man's limitations cannot be avoided when a writer examines man's wholeness. White follows the lead that German psychologists presented as Gestalt theory. The French anthropologists more recently called it "total entity."

White writes about people most novelists pass by. His characters only seem to be ordinary folk. Actually, they have a lively feeling about the mystery and complexity of life that is extraordinary. As we shall see when we examine the leading figures of his books, his characters are not developed; they are revealed.

Today Australians are being made to face a complex world for which their way of life and literature ill prepared them. This partially explains their hesitancy to accept Patrick White. Confused themselves, Australians have often found White's characters confusing and unflattering. In novel after novel, White has extended the limits of accepted literary content. In particular, *The Eye of the Storm* is an enlarging and sometimes shocking experience. Remembering that Australia was once a subcontinent freed from a mainland, White borrows from the *Rig Veda* story the idea of the "freeing of the waters." He sees Australia as "tomorrow land."

INTRODUCTION TO THE EYE OF THE STORM

THEMES

The chief **theme** is the quest for the meaning of love, but not in the simple sense of "boy meets girl." Instead love is revealed as a progression or becoming. It moves and grows from one universal aspect to another. There are four stages, each stage becoming a section of this twelve-chapter book. In using twelve chapters with four divisions, White shows his familiarity with the traditional literary structure of the quaternary. He had used it with success in earlier novels. In this one, the division into four is more subtle, one section flowing into the next in easy transition. It would seem, however, that each three-chapter block has a dominant symbol around which other lesser symbols are arranged. The lesser symbols often repeat in all of the sections. Each section may also be said to have a prevailing color. The minor colors are repeated in all sections because in a sense each character has an identifying color, regardless of varying degrees of tonal value. At the same time it must be remembered that Patrick White is not above inverting his symbols. He enjoys playing tricks on his readers in the same way that his characters sometimes subconsciously play tricks on themselves. In this way their characteristics emerge.

Among the novel's many secondary themes, four stand out. All of these are aspects of the traditional motif of "sight." The first of these deals with the struggle between honesty and dishonesty - how one sees oneself - how honest one is - how honest others are - the number of times the same person is honest compared with the times dishonest. The next concerns the method of sight. Mrs. Hunter is nearly blind. Her half-sight puts her in the category of the legendary. "Among the blind the one-eyed is king." Here the queen dominates those with 20/20 vision. The third **theme** deals with the thin wavering line between reality and illusion. When is the illusory most real? This is the question begun by White in his early novel, *The Aunt's Story* and explored by him ever since. White seems to be saying what the mind can see is real. The last quarter takes up the "Tiresias" **theme**. In Greek mythology Tiresias was blinded by Athene because he saw her in the bath. Later the goddess partially forgave him by bestowing upon him the power of "second sight," the gift of prophecy. Unfortunately this ability has its dark side. It may be a curse. Accordingly, the **theme** widens into the concept that without evil there can be no good. It is necessary to be able to "see" evil. It must also be remembered that in one version of the Tiresias myth the soothsayer was first transformed into a woman then back into a man. Thus the Tiresias good-and-evil motif is tied into the main **theme** of love and love is always blind.

Other lesser **themes** include the Phoenix myth, the Vernal Equinox, fertility, the renewal in Passover and Easter, the Promethean myth of man against God, the story of Adam who carried Eve within his rib, the story of the Grail, and many other ancient **themes** in modern dress. White's use of the tried and true archetypes is not stale because he often inverts or parodies them imaginatively. Through them we can absorb more and more of what this novel can teach us.

SYMBOLS

Words are symbols. Just as in mathematical games, we "let x" stand for something, usually an unknown quantity, words stand for something - things, or functions, animate, or inanimate - in many categories themselves all named and symbolic. It is a great game and Patrick White is a professional game player. All in fun we take games seriously. White frequently uses x to express y - which is **metaphor** the use of one word to express another. Words are not used for words' sake but to brighten intelligibility. Words don't dress up thought but are co-efficients of thought. This multi-functional mode of expression transmits experience economically. A secondary layer of language penetrates the reader's consciousness.

Like any artist, trying to create a structure, and he conceives the novel as a structure, White is both a problem solver and a presenter of new problems which demand solution. He is among those who react to the problems of our times in an entirely personal way. In speaking through the mouths of his characters he is able to avoid making judgments. He condemns no one, not even those he satirizes as the living dead - the unaware. His sense of humor is never far from the surface. Sometimes we feel he plays a version of Blindman's Bluff. He follows Wittgenstein in making a distinction between "spiel," playing, and "ernst," playing a game. Playing a game involves rules which in turn suggest the possibility of cheating. As White's words break many grammatical rules, so his characters can be caught cheating. Perhaps this is what makes them human. But let it be said that though White plays with words, he never cheats his readers. We can trust him to "tell it like it is," humorously but not sentimentally.

THE EYE OF THE STORM

TEXTUAL ANALYSIS

CHAPTER ONE

PROGRESSION OF STORY

The prevailing symbol of Chapter One is the mirror. Those of us who remember Nathaniel Hawthorne's *Scarlet Letter* know that the mirror symbol is not new. Yet how different is the great sun of a mirror that White centers in the rosewood headboard of Mrs. Hunter's great bed. She knew how it and the room's many other mirrors annoyed the visitors to her sick room. And let us not forget the partly covered bed pan with the glare shining on its immaculate surface.

REFLECTIONS

The glimpses that we get by way of introduction to the novel's leading characters are passing but revealing reflections. They appear with what the portrait painter, Van Gogh, called "terrifying lucidity." When the night nurse tilts the looking glass for Elizabeth to have a look at herself, she is glad her patient has dim eyes. In this one bit of opening action, we learn several things with immediacy; Mrs. Hunter is vain, she deceives herself, knows she does upon reflection, and that the nurse, Marie de Santis is sympathetic. A few pages later when the nurse descends in the lower caverns of the house to get some fresh water (itself a symbol), she passes a great gilded mirror. To get away from what she sees she steps into the drawing room where the family portraits hang - an artist's reflection of an earlier time. Here we see a youthful, beautiful Mrs. Hunter in evening dress with diamonds on her shoulders and wrists. In an almost unbelievably short time White has merged the past with the present. We learn not only more about the sick old woman upstairs but something of her two children with whom she was painted. We see these two as "then" before we see them as "now." The little girl, whom the nurse was soon to meet as the Princess de Lascabanes, is here prejudged as gloomy and the little boy who was to become the famous actor, knighted by royalty, Sir Basil Hunter, is a spiteful looking child.

ONOMASTICS

Here we must examine the names of the characters we have already met. White's use of onomastics, the selection of names to denote personality, begun in earlier novels where it was occasionally criticized as unnecessary, is here used with greater subtlety. Hunter was Elizabeth's married name. (Her husband, no hunter in the physical sense of killing prey, was a hunter in the searcher/seeker sense.) The name Elizabeth reveals the queen, the alert, the schemer, the royal personage. The two children, born Hunter, are amalgams of their parents. Dorothy, when spelled Dorothea, is a turnaround of Theodora, or gift of God. Some readers may here exclaim "what a gift!" Lascabanes, the

Frenchman who gave her his name, is certainly of a "scabrous" family whose nastiness seems to have been contagious. The Hunter boy's name, Basil, has more than one **connotation**. Basil is well known in the kitchen as a spice. He surely brings spice to the novel. More subtly, continuing in White's multi-lingual vein, Basil is French: bas meaning low and ill, the masculine pronoun. The masculinity of the name is ironic in the character's affinity with Adam, Tiresias, Oedipus, and Lord Byron.

We have also met Mary de Santis. The custom of calling a nurse "sister" is English and by transfer Australian. By giving the name Mary to the night nurse, and not to her morning or afternoon counterparts, White adds the peace and quiet, usually associated with darkness, to the holy name. The mysticism of the stars and sky, the early dawn, is implied. She is the dark-haired one who we suspect will soon be grey. And, of course, she is a virgin, though full-breasted. White gives her the last name de Santis which implies saintliness but does not necessarily mean she is consistently saintly. Her prim blue sailor hat gets changed for an orange-colored creation on her date with Sir Basil. It is also to be noted that White calls her a high priestess, even an arch priestess. This suggests she is merely a servant who approaches sanctity.

DREAMS THAT REVEAL

There is still another technique by which the author introduces his characters - a technique we shall observe in every chapter. It seems that White never stops "introducing" his characters. We can be more than half way through the story when a new piece is fitted into the puzzlement that each of the main figures is. Only the pieces on the outer rim, the frame as it were, are sorted out in the first chapter. The technique used presents tell-tale bits of drama, including the dreams, day-dreams, and spoken reminiscences of his people. For example, before Sister Mary de Santis reaches the kitchen, Mrs. Hunter has slipped off into a half-dozen about the dolls of her childhood. We learn that they were not her dolls but a friend's. Her own family was too poor for dolls. More importantly we learn that the child Elizabeth had pulled the legs off the dolls. And as dreams flit from one event to the next, we learn some more about her husband Alfred - that men and women liked him because he could fool them with gruff talk. Neither sex knew how immaculate he was. We are being given a taste of White's **irony**. Those who suspected her of being the "cold one" of the partnership are classed with those unaware people whom White can chop to pieces. Revealed also is the knowledge that Elizabeth Hunter enjoyed other lovers. One is mentioned, Athol Shreve. The name itself is predictive of enlargement. There is enough of a suggestion of Dublin in it to make us sense the Joycean scene White later burlesques. The other man in her fleeting dream is not named, perhaps to add pique and importance to the Norwegian figure appearing in the novel's title scene of the storm. His being mentioned in Chapter One, and being kept alive by some reference or other in every subsequent chapter, is linked to another symbol, so briefly one is apt to miss it - the symbol of the fish which later becomes dominant.

REMINISCENCES THAT REVEAL

It is also to be noted that Mrs. Hunter is not the only information giver. Mary de Santis introduces the solicitor, Arnold Wyburd. (Note last name and also that Arnold is related to the French Arnault, and further back to the Greek, meaning, here ironically, "strong as an eagle.") By a reminiscence once removed we learn two more pieces; one that Wyburd had recommended the nurse because she had been faithful to an ex-colonel who had left her a small inheritance, secondly, that Wyburd had recommended his client, Mrs. Hunter, for her delight in battles of wit.

FROM ILLUSION TO REALITY

White's skill in putting his actors on stage is second only to that of another disclosure concerning the book's **theme**. It transpires when White makes the transition at the end of Mrs. Hunter's dream to the reality of the nurse's errand for the glass of water. The old lady doesn't want to dream any further about family and lovers; she wants to think about something more meaningful - she wants to find a state of mind where she can experience something new, something never yet brought to her long life. Here White is both challenging the reader to ask himself what it is that the old woman still wants and also stating the truth of the old **cliche**, "where there's life...."

THEME THROUGH SYMBOL

There is a further hint that White is telling us that in her experience of the eye of the storm, Mrs. Hunter failed to fathom all of its meaning. Before she slips from reality again we see the ancient soul sucking the corner of her bed-pillow. Then when the nurse brings the water, we view the toothless old mouth sucking from the glass like a fish. The symbol of sucking is an exaggeration of any number of extracting symbols which imply that more may be extracted. This use of exaggeration on the part of the author accentuates his dramatic sense. In this same chapter the sucking symbol is inverted into a funnel suggestive of a cyclone's twister. White's frequent inversion of symbols is typical and should be watched because they not only amaze the reader but enlighten him. Each time the sucking symbol is repeated the **metaphor** receives a change. Here the funnel shifts the concept of what might be sucked in to that which is or has been actually poured in. When the day nurse pours the delicious coffee into Mrs. Hunter, we feel that she is not only sensuously and physically pleased but also that she is capable of being fed perhaps even spiritual food. We have moved from the present of what is happening to what might happen. By this simple action of coffee drinking, the author has manipulated time which loses tense.

DISCLOSURE THROUGH THE SENSES

Still introducing his leading characters, White once again takes us backward. He uses different degrees of the senses of touch, sound, and smell. The lawyer Wyburd is being presented. Elizabeth touches his hand which seems paper-thin, dry like his voice. She smells him and asks him to take off his coat. These physical reactions on her part turn her mind away from the smells of rubbing alcohol and baby powder back into the past. She sees Wyburd as he had, years before, stood naked before her in the same room, shy before the same mirrors. The sexy reminiscence or dream that teaches us much about the participants is identified by a symbol, a physical characteristic. Wyburd's body was nearly hairless, a bit of description easily missed. In Elizabeth's subsequent encounters with men, the degree of their hairiness determines their strength if not their importance. White uses hair as signal. It alerts the reader to what is coming. Its use is a part of White's genius for creating suspense.

DISCLOSURE THROUGH CONTRAST

The identification of a character by an unforgettable feature is but a part of White's method of contrasting his people. We learn about the differences between mother and daughter not through the words of an omniscient author but through action. We have Elizabeth Hunter act with the nurses and act with Wyburd and then we observe Dorothy act. The sad part is that she does not act like her mother with others. As a girl she snooped in the maids' rooms for signs of sex. Here she revisits her own room and writhes sensuously on her old bed. She is alone and lonely. The contrast to her mother is sharp. Yet she is her mother's flesh and blood. She is voluptuous. Here the reader's curiosity is aroused again by the suggestion that perhaps the sensuous old woman is to become lonely and the lonely daughter sensuous. The plot thickens through a combination of character revelation, signal, **metaphor** and symbol.

DISCLOSURE THROUGH COLOR

The question of the domination of a certain color in the opening quarter is still unsettled. That no single color is firmed up is part of the gradualness of the character disclosure. White is the color of the sick room attendants. With Mary de Santis' white veil or cap, virgin blue is also associated. With the afternoon day nurse, Florrie Manhood (note name), the rubbing thighs beneath her starched skirt are linked with the bright prints of her off-duty clothes. Manhood has a life beyond the sick room whereas de Santis has little or none. Then we have the white dresses Elizabeth wears in her dreams. They are here and continue to be signals of intimacy.

On the other hand, the white of the opening quarter turns occasionally to gold. De Santis in Chapter Three uses a gold pen while writing in the early dawn. Mrs. Hunter's skin is ivory colored. We also have the colors of the dresser set, particularly the mirror, framed in ivory, gold, and blue lapis. The jewel case has its tricky lock. White piles up the symbolism by showing Mrs. Hunter as a lock-opener, first of material things, then spiritual. The jewels jumbled within the case are many colored. A sinister sense of touch is added when rings turn fingers into claws. A weird Ethiopian jewel, given by Basil to his mother, is worn on a thumb.

THEME THROUGH COLOR

As color is used in character revelation, so also is it used to develop **theme**. In sharp contrast to her mother, the Princess Dorothy is a colorless person. Her clothes, though expensive, are not new. They are apt to be black and economical. Her mother is flamboyant and extravagant. Dorothy's simple Lanvin gown can be made over again and again with perhaps a change of jewelry, colorless pearls for example. One feels that the daughter is a warmed over person, whereas the mother is forever warming up. Their personalities clash from the moment Dorothy rushes awkwardly into the sick room. Her intended embrace is foiled by the thermometer stuck in her mother's mouth. Attempts at conversation never blossom. The old lady soon lapses into a colorful dream about a canary. The not so young daughter remembers a Dutchman with square hands who had sat next to her on the plane from Paris. But nothing came of the incident, even though they ran into a storm and he told her of a cyclone (suggestive of Mrs. Hunter's experience). Mrs. Hunter, one feels, would not let the chance for a flirtation slip from her as it did Dorothy, hugging her colorless Persian lamb coat.

DISCLOSURE THROUGH STYLE

The flatness of the passage is offset by its humor, caused by the fact that no one, the old woman, the nurse, the lawyer, then the doctor (appropriately named Gidley), understands the other, except Mrs. Hunter and the doctor whom she later admits she might have enjoyed as a lover. The passage also contains a piece of writing that is linguistically challenging and revealing. An example of what has been called White's "awful parentheses" occurs on the top of page 59 of the Avon paperback edition. If either of the two women had entertained the thought expressed, there would have been no need for the parentheses. It would merely have been a non-Patrick White example of interior monologue. By beginning with "they" instead of "I," the author has telescoped the interiors of two people, in a way that might be called interior dialogue. However, this label would be inaccurate because the telescoping is further extended by the shift from "they" to "you," which may be singular or plural. Secondly, "you" is not the impersonal "one" which is grammatically strictly singular. The "you" of the last clause forces the reader to include himself in the thought. Unknowingly the reader has had an experience that is either new or at least re-enforced. This is the kind of writing that has contributed to White's canon. We shall come upon more of the same. The thought of the passage that you cannot always be sure whether people love you or hate you is also one of the novel's subsidiary themes.

THE EYE OF THE STORM

TEXTUAL ANALYSIS

CHAPTER TWO

TRUTH AND THE SICKROOM

In Chapter Two White, through the revelations of his characters, continues his search into new sources of truth. The secrets of the sickroom continue to reveal. Dostoyevsky exploited it in the *Brothers Karamazov*, Tolstoy even more brilliantly in the death of Levin's brother in *Anna Karenina*, and Flaubert in Emma Bovary's death in *Madame Bovary*. With White the smelly and unsightly details are eclipsed by his perception into the heart, mind, and soul of the patient. He points out that one of the by-products of being bedridden is boredom. However, it is not the monotony of the day in and day out that White presents. Instead, he stresses the patient's former boredom and uses it to advance his story. Mrs. Hunter was bored with the half-dead acquaintances of her youth, bored with her sheep-raising misfit of a husband, bored with her children, bored as a motherless widow, bored by her increasing possessions. Yet what alerts the reader is White's implication of the lengths that Mrs. Hunter went to overcome her perhaps sinful ennui. White's genius for creating suspense puts action into the fixed state of invalidism.

TRUTH AND OLD AGE

Though King Lear remains classic in this area of literature, White adds to the **genre**. It was no accident that one reviewer called Elizabeth Hunter, "Mrs. Lear." The comparison is both clever and inexact. She more nearly resembles Lear's reflection in the person of Gloucester whose physical and psychic blindness kept him from understanding his two sons. So Mrs. Hunter failed with her two children. Also it must be recalled that Lear divested himself of his possessions. By contrast Queen Hunter was anxious for more; she wanted to possess a new experience.

THEME THROUGH ENLARGEMENT

In this chapter White's **theme** advances by the enlargement of three powerful ingredients - pathos, **satire**, and bawdy humor. At the same time two new important characters are added, the afternoon nurse and the housekeeper, both with revelatory names; the first Florrie Manhood with her florid prints, bright lipstick and a weakness for the opposite sex; the second, Lottie Lipmann (lot a lip) once aggressive, determined, courageous, a cabaret artiste who deserted her man because she was a Jewess and so might endanger her Aryan lover in Nazi Germany. These two women and Mrs. Hunter form the pathetic trio of Lorrie, Lottie, and 'Lizbeth. All three are potential "tear-jerkers" made interesting by White because of their differences. They have contrasting views of life and death. Florrie, the one driven by her desires, whose capacity for love is never filled, wants only contentment from life. Lottie, whose lot has been to lose those she loves, has been drained by love. She is tired of life. 'Lizbeth, loved but not loving, is determined to get an experience out of making a gift of love even if it kills her. Mrs. Hunter is also a combination of the other two. She recognizes in Florrie Manhood her own youthful urges and in the complete selflessness of Lottie's undemanding love she senses what she failed at. There is a good deal of movement in these three figures. The nurse's brisk attention to duty and her energetic lovemaking, and the housekeeper's "one, two, three dancing" with or without benefit of costume, are reflected in the lively jumps in the invalid's thoughts. Coupled with her gulping mouth and clawing hands they make the relationships of these three the most kinetic of any in the novel.

COMIC RELIEF

The three are also the kingpins (queenpins) on which White fastens his brightest **satire**. He makes fun of Lorrie's man friend whom Mrs. Hunter can smell when her nurse has been with him. He satirizes Col Pardoe as a type of Australian youth who make use of their girls. Florrie fries his mutton chops, either at her place or his place. He reads books, uses words not in her vocabulary, plays classical records, mood music for lovemaking, drives a sporty but second-hand car, works in a drugstore, and likes his days off. The housekeeper's dancing, whose style changes later, is a satiric mime on Nazi cruelty and grossness. Her dressing up in the shoddy black suit and battered top hat is a **burlesque** that undresses the puny emotions of the fearful. The jars and tubes used in the making up of the ancient crone are a **satire** on skin-deep beauty. The roseate gown, the moth-eaten sable, and the lilac wig are tools of **satire**. The **irony** rests in the fact that, though the illusion of beauty fails, the reality of the love of the two acolytes for their employer is truly beautiful - but not sentimental.

PROPHECY THROUGH HUMOR

Manhood is quite capable of calling Mrs. Hunter the "old bitch" of Moreton (more tone) Drive and Mrs. Hunter can bawl her out for not sticking her false teeth in under the carnation lipstick. White's **theme** of comparing the reality of illusion and illusion of reality is advancing with humor and prophecy. When the "old bag" upstairs wonders why more patients are not murdered by their nurses who almost rub them out of existence with baths of wood alcohol, we are forewarned of the suggestion of mercy killing that later horrifies the nurse. Meanwhile the sickroom fumes are sprayed with healthy humor. There can be no blushes between nurse and patient. White invades their privacy with puns, sarcasm, and repeated metaphors, including the funnel. There can be no question that in this chapter White has made a new symbol out of dreck. (There were suggestions of its symbolic value in his preceding novel, *The Vivisector*.) From a structural viewpoint it serves as a unifying element not to be ignored.

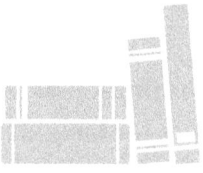

THE EYE OF THE STORM

TEXTUAL ANALYSIS

CHAPTER THREE

MULTI-LEVEL READING

Chapter Three is important because it points up the necessity of reading Patrick White on more than one level. Its hotel bedroom scene has been criticized as exceeding the limits of what a serious novel should contain. This may be prudery. On the other hand to read it only as a juicy tale in the tradition of Chaucer or Boccaccio is equally puerile. We must remember that this chapter is still introducing Mrs. Hunter's son Basil.

STYLE AND THEME

The color of Basil is green. Sir Basil is a distinguished actor known in every English green room. We see him as a middle-aged roue, still green. Unfortunately his budding has never matured. He is a lonely soul whom White presents with all the stage business of bawdy humor. Ironically, he can sow a seed or two in the reader's mind. Remembering that White is also a playwright, we can appreciate here how well the style of the stage is fused with theme.

PHILOSOPHY AND THEME

In surrounding Basil, a major character in the novel, with the minor actors he meets on his stopover in Bangkok, White exaggerates the extremes of the beautiful and the ugly, the spiritual and the worldly not only within the same person in the same **episode** but in relationship to the novel's other major figures. The young woman who draws the drunken Basil into Bangkok's Miramar, room 365, may be related to his mother's ex-actress housekeeper, Lottie Lipmann. The ingenue becomes a nihilist when compared to the selfless older woman. She wants to experience everything, even to the experience of a distasteful older man, like Sir Basil. We feel that, in her desire to eat up the world, she is indeed carrying on a dialogue with nothingness. In order to act a part she pitifully seeks the truth within people without knowing that truth also exists between people. Lottie Lipmann, who has perhaps experienced too much, dresses up, dances, and puts on an act to create for herself an illusion. "Pretending" is a need deep within her. She needs an outlet for her emotions. When this actress/ex-actress serves her German noodle soup to Sir Basil, the actor who has played Lear and now wants to play "himself," she calls out to him from the depths, "If I could begin again."

ART AND THEME

Lottie is the artist. She explains that she wants to create something with her acting - one whole human being. For a moment in our reading, we feel we are listening to the voice of Patrick White. Also we are aware that the author in this last chapter of the first quarter is introducing a second **theme** or at least a variation on Mrs. Hunter's theme of wanting to find a new kind of love. Finding love through creation is a universal desire expressed here by Lottie's attempt to create something, even soup, for a fellow actor, Sir Basil. It is interesting that White presents this scene with Lottie before the actor remembers what happened in Bangkok.

THE EYE OF THE STORM

TEXTUAL ANALYSIS

CHAPTER FOUR

ENVIRONMENTAL THEME

In the opening chapter of the novel's second quarter, "windows" are the leading symbol. Windows are see-throughs. The main characters are beginning to be more perceptive of each other. If at first they seemed loveless, hateful and punitive, here they evoke a certain sympathy in the reader. White reveals them from a different perspective. He introduces us, at the same time, to Sydney, Australia, and a section of its life psychologically and economically apart from the windows open to the gardens of Moreton Drive. The windows down Botany Way reflect the blazes shooting from the stinking oil refineries. In this chapter we see characters from the viewpoint of environment rather than heredity.

ENVIRONMENT AND LANGUAGE

There is a shift in writing style to go with the shift in content. We become more aware of White's genius in the management of language. As we had a raucous scene in Bangkok where the actors were all English, we now have a glimpse of Australian slum life with Australian expressions. As we had **satire** upon the mansion's cloakroom toilet that wouldn't flush and its link to Mrs. Hunter's worn out plumbing, we now can smell the stench of grease and gin in working people's walk-up flats. White has a fine ear for the language of the common folk. They contrast, beneficially, with their sometimes superficially more refined counterparts. They contrast with Mrs. Hunter's whites and blues and compare with the green of Basil and the traveling troupe. But, in characteristic White fashion, mutations occur. We see these Australians as a young people, still a bit raw, unsentimentalized by White. Nevertheless, there is a sickness in their health. It is sad but also ironically commendable that the concrete walk in front of the Vidlers' had been colored green. White's propensity for revealing names continues with Florrie Manhood's landlords Vid and Viddie (the seeing ones, continuing the window **metaphor**, yet with blinkers, blinds). In giving the name Snow to Florrie's cousin who had been white-haired from adolescence, White's **satire** on purity contrasts with his satire on the same quality in the upper class. Snow's lack of it and her perversion of love is made blatant in White's use of smutty language.

ENVIRONMENT AND STRUCTURE

However, the author's **satire** here is less vitriolic than that dealt out to those who are perhaps responsible for Sydney's slums. There is even a kindness in Snow's remark in connection with her cousin Florrie's patient, that it might be better if old people were turned over to incinerators. Her comment, tied to White's sickroom descriptions, makes us aware how White never loses track of his main theme and his consciousness of the novel's structure. His suggestions to the reader never fail with changes in style or content. White keeps asking what is wrong with modern civilization. Why can't windows be opened up?

As to the colors of this chapter, they are still variegated, coming close to the cretonne of Snow's dinette bench. Flo's orange bag, the crimson of the store signs, the pink beads of a lampshade, and the blue eye-shadow of make-up rival the fluorescence of flaming nail polish. The settlers of Australia are still unsettled.

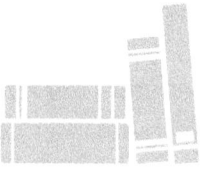

THE EYE OF THE STORM

TEXTUAL ANALYSIS

CHAPTER FIVE

VARIATIONS ON THE TRADITIONAL

In the fifth chapter, certain features of White's style are clearly recognizable. Certain traditional elements are subtly varied under White's management. For example, White's use of letter-writing, which in past fiction revealed the character of the letter-writer and also moved the plot forward, here not only serves these purposes but also becomes a method of prophecy. The reader may recall the arrival of two letters, one from each of the two Hunter children at Kudjeri. Mrs. Hunter in her half-dream remembered she had gone there to be with her husband on his death bed. White has swung the clock around from the present deep into the past and then into the future. The action of the image is circular. Mrs. Hunter is dreaming of the two old letters which alert the reader to events that are still to come. This movement is typical of White's use of "prolepsis," defined in rhetoric as "the anticipation and answering of an objection or argument before one's opponent has put it forward." In White's utilization the participating reader is often an "opponent." At this point White admits that the reader is in opposition to what he already guesses the two Hunter children are about to do to their mother.

WINNING THE READER

By contrast the return to Kudjeri is used to make us dislike Mrs. Hunter less. We see her being kind to her husband. She is capable of small loving attentions hardly to be imagined of the character in Chapter One. She has "developed" since the opening but in White fashion her development took place prior to the present, a time that was, however, responsible for her present condition. Her desire for some new experience was prophesied when, knowing that her husband was dying, she sent the doctor away. She was not afraid to be alone then as she was not to be afraid later when alone in the eye of the storm. She wanted to share the mystery her husband was about to experience. She wanted to participate in what she thought was a miracle - the soul's escape from the body.

METAPHORIC OVERTONES

After presenting this story of emotional release as one of Mrs. Hunter's recollections, White writes a descant above it in the shape of an **episode** that takes place while Mrs. Hunter is doing her apocalyptic remembering. Sister Mary de Santis had gone below to the kitchen and scrubbed the already clean floor. She seemed subconsciously to want a release from her night thoughts. White's metaphoric use of water and soap suds to wash away one's troubles is doubled here by the jerking back and forth of the nurse's white cap and the swinging of her full breasts over the glistening linoleum.

POETIC EPIPHANY

The above excellent piece of writing is followed by a passage that is even more meaningful. The style is suitably poetic. Sister Mary had gone into the garden and collected roses still moist in the early dawn. Through the fence she had become aware of a passer-by who had stopped to ask directions. (The reader at this point may be reminded of the famous Joycean epiphany in *The Portrait of the Artist as a Young Man* where Stephen asks his way of a flower vendor.) The encounter here contains one of White's most striking observations. When the man had asked the nurse if anyone was sick and on being told that an old lady was, he compares life in old age with an electric light bulb going on and off occasionally showing up something new. In this ironic epiphany White is once more being prophetic; light beams from the blind.

PHILOSOPHIC PUNNING

Even when most serious, White is unable to resist a bit of word play; for example, the pun included in Mrs. Hunter's reverie about the end of life: she is revealed as believing that death should not be painless or easy, but rather the "highest, the most difficult peak of all." The "high" concept is extended by the word "peak" which is surely a pun as a "peek" into heaven. A bit further on, when Mrs. Hunter answers the nurse's admonition that she would wake herself up if she talked too much, the invalid responded with the remark that only sleep woke her up. This typically Whitean twist implies that by "sleep" she meant death. She expected that death would wake her up...would be an experience.

THE EYE OF THE STORM

TEXTUAL ANALYSIS

CHAPTER SIX

STAGE MANAGEMENT

Upon reflection this last chapter of the first half of the novel tells us much about Patrick White and his technique. Certain elements are apt to be missed as we rush on with the story. This is regrettable. Part of the enjoyment of the novel stems from an awareness of the particular "mix" that is Patrick White. In this chapter he seems to start off as a dramatist and to wind up as a painter/poet. Like Shakespeare, White tumbles at least seven distinct scenes into a single act. In the first four, Dorothy plays center stage. By the novelist's technique of juxtaposition, the last three are played by Basil. With a bow to Virginia Woolf, White turns Elizabethan soliloquy into interior monologue.

PSYCHOLOGY OF DREAMS

White's differences are more noteworthy than his similarities to his predecessors. Dorothy's scene is what modern analysts might call a "rev" dream. After eating her Australian mutton chops, long out of fashion in her French continental diet, the princess' after-dinner doze varies with the depth of her sleep. She does not speak her lines. The jade grey area of her mind is described by White in vivid, if ungrammatical terms. Brumby Island, forecasting the storm to come, the rain forest, wild horses, flying sand precede the nightmarish flashes. She could kill her mother. Then Wyburd, the nasty old lawyer, makes his dream appearance, blue-veined and naked.

White mirrors the dream in the bent glass reflections of a circus gallery. Distortions do not conceal the subject. Nevertheless, White is not an omniscient author, determined on making an assessment of Dorothy. The shorthand language used to describe the dream suggests a mode of thought. Dorothy's way of thinking is expressed in her own manner, not in White's more characteristically symbolic stance.

The shift in style of the later scene in which Basil talks to himself is interrupted by the comic relief of the wide-awake telephone conversation Dorothy has when her old friend, Cherry Cheeseman, invites her to dinner. Double meanings abound when the two exchange their civilities. The false, the banal, even the indelicate, turn the telephone instruments into echoing tunnels. White's repeated metaphoric use of tunnels and funnels is used here in a harsh diagnosis of Australian affluent society. As a native son, White feels he has the right to find fault. He can poke fun in ways he would disallow others outside the family boundaries. D. H. Lawrence spent three months in Australia and was critical, paid a left-handed compliment when he found

Australia refreshing after London's "horrible stuffiness." One of the **themes** of his novel *Kangaroo* is the absence in Australia of an "inner life." White's familiarity with Sydney makes him know in greater detail what Lawrence was trying to say. In *Cherry Cheeseman* he treats Australia with humor and thereby provides transition to an introduction to Basil's monologue out of Picadilly.

THE WORLD IS NOT A STAGE

Dorothy has a dream but Sir Basil talks to himself. White modulates to a different key even though the words of daydreams rush on without the benefit of **syntax**. Basil's ruminations upon his boyhood are witnesses of White's concept of time as immeasurable by an hour glass. For this scene he places Sir Basil center stage, seated on a park bench where he examines a blade of grass. Though his thought hurtles to his affair with Mitty Jacka and her determination to write a play where he would play "himself," we are always aware of the restless doubts nagging the aging actor. White is gradually revealing a character with whom we can sympathize. Basil knows the drama he is playing for his mother, his sister, the lawyer, and the nurses is "unplayable." He is aware how the techniques of the theater have made him dishonest.

PAINT AND GREASE PAINT

Patrick White seems to be expressing a personal fear that the legerdemain of his own brilliant writing may compromise honesty. As Lord Byron admitted himself to be a compulsive writer, so seems Patrick White. Words spring from inner necessity. The artist is driven. Basil, Elizabeth Hunter's son, is an actor driven. He is an artist, "malgre lui," in spite of himself. As White portrayed the artist-painter in Hurtle Duffield in *The Vivisector*, the novel just previous to this one, he here paints the artist-actor. What remains most interesting is the complete change in heredity and environment of the **protagonists** while in each a similar creative sensibility is maintained. This is another element in the White canon.

THE EYE OF THE STORM

TEXTUAL ANALYSIS

CHAPTER SEVEN

OUTWORN LABELS

An examination of the "set comic pieces" of this chapter shows how White varies what some critics lump together as a set characteristic. The first to be looked at is the tableau of the Cheeseman dinner. The labels of **Realism** and Naturalism are dangerously inexact. The details of what the guests wore, their hosts' furniture and powder rooms may be summed up as White's reaction to the writing of a hundred years ago. Today we expect our authors to be more precise than shocking. We accept the man that Naturalism debased. The aesthetic appeal grows from the selectivity of the precision. Photographic verisimilitude must also be imaginative. What makes the Cheeseman dinner both raucously funny and a sad commentary is a display of writing genius. The author's perception of what lies under the pink and blue decolletage, of what is missing in the pseudo-antiques, and of what secrets are hid in the powder room relates the factual to the imaginative. White's use of **irony**, sarcasm, **burlesque**, puns, and metaphors of sight (colors) and taste (rich food) is stylistically accurate.

COMIC CATHARSIS

The next big scene is noteworthy for what it does to the actors. Florrie Manhood and Sir Basil are changed people after their brief union. The nurse who thought she wanted a child of a better background than Col Pardoe's is relieved when she learns she is not pregnant. Basil, always seeking fulfillment in a new sexual encounter, discovers that the best of such can only make him more aware of his loneliness.

THE RANGE OF REFERENCE

In describing the loneliness of these two people, White is returning to a **theme** ever present in his novels. Here it is refreshed by the ironic fact that they were most acutely alone when they were together. With this enlargement of meaning his **theme** has grown. Recalling the earlier scene of Sir Basil's meeting with one of the actresses in the troupe in Bangkok, we realize how different this **episode** is. There sex is secondary to the liquor and gaiety of the party. Here the sex is primary and highlighted by White's recurrent symbolism. Hairiness is again an opening signal. Water suggests the "cleansing" that is about to occur. Sir Basil, just out of a shower, opens the door to Florrie with but a towel wrapped about him. Basil, so sure of himself as a possessor, turns out to be possessed. This is a typical White and twist flourishing irresistibly with his delicious sense of humor and salty language.

COMIC IRONY

There is a decided transition period before the chapter's last comic piece. It contains a bit of writing that is both subtle and ironic. Once again color **metaphors** are in the foreground. On her return to Elizabeth Hunter's bed side, Florrie is asked to bring out the jewel box. The old lady wants to give her nurse a sapphire ring to mark her engagement to Col Pardoe. The sapphire must be a pink one, not blue. Pink was feminine; blue too spiritual. As if he could not contain the **satire** any further, White has Florrie explode with the remark that she might turn out to be an old maid. Then both women laughed. This interim piece is actually funnier than the "set" comedy that preceded and that which follows.

PROPHETIC COMEDY

By her visit to her employer's son, Sister Mary de Santis hoped to do something good. In his turn Sir Basil invited her to lunch. He too wanted to do good. That neither was successful is the result of a comedy of errors starting with the nurse's new orange hat and concluding with the traffic jam in downtown Sydney. At the luncheon in the bayside restaurant, sex is either a controlled undertone or a raucous descant provided by other diners. The contrast between our pair and their unknown table neighbors is marked. White relates the unrelated with gusto. The scene is slapstick. The sensuality limited at first to food (again a recurrent **metaphor**) later suggests obscenity. It turns completely sour with the appearance of the dead dog floating up the beach. The scene is no longer funny. The good intentions with which Sister Mary and Sir Basil started the day vanish in the fumes. However, in the author's technique of reversal we see how precisely he has further revealed his characters. Spiritually and intellectually, they began the day apart. By noon with the help of food and drink they approached a certain intimacy. By evening their separateness was accentuated. The two women, Florrie Manhood and Sister Mary, akin in their loneliness, different in their desires, had, we sense, basically the same effect on Basil. When the reader feels their commonality, the author is prophesying another time when they will join in a common action. The technique of prolepsis is recognizable.

PURGATION SYMBOLS

Discussion of this chapter cannot be closed without calling attention to the recurrent references to purgation at critical points. They reveal much about the book's characters and structurally they advance and connect several minor themes. The following may be located:

1. When, on his way up to Elizabeth's room, Wyburd is reminded by Lottie Lipmann that the cloakroom lavatory would not spill - flush.

2. When at the Cheeseman dinner, Doug livens up the Princess' plate with the parson's nose.

3. When after the same dinner the ladies withdraw to powder their noses. Mrs. Cheeseman leads them back to join the men. Her retinue of women had told secrets, blushed, and flushed.

4. When Lottie Lipmann explains to Badgery that she had burnt the strudel because of the arrival of the plumber

who had to unblock the cloakroom lavatory, Badgery insists it was not her fault.

5. When Mary de Santis lifts her patient onto the commode, Mrs. Hunter says that nurses hanging around, treating one like dirt, cause constipation.

6. When at the restaurant by the seaside, the beach is lapped by scum and feces.

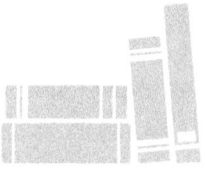

THE EYE OF THE STORM

TEXTUAL ANALYSIS

CHAPTER EIGHT

| SO WHAT

Chapter Eight can be reread with profit, not only for its description of the cyclone which gives the novel its title, but also for the questions it poses. Up to this point we have been examining how the author introduces his characters, how his **themes** are structured, and how he uses language. Now we must ask why and to what purpose. If at one point or another we have suggested a meaning, there has always been the possibility that meaning might be something else. Patrick White may have been stretching our minds. Now he sets limits. At the outset the story progressed as if the author had no claim on the reader. We evaluated the novel regardless of any intention of the author. This has been proper. Now the question is, have our efforts been worthwhile?

MORAL NEUTRALISM

It has been pointed out that White, in speaking through his characters, has shown them ancestrally and environmentally as they are, or at least as they appear to each other. He has compared, he has developed the less obvious and even made fun but he has not said what is good or bad. What White finds significant in each character is about to change in emphasis so that the personal judgments the reader has been making are about to shift. To sum up, Mrs. Hunter has most likely been judged a once beautiful vain woman, unsatisfied, incomplete, learning much from life but always asking for more and more. We know that she had lived through a storm that had tested her endurance to the limit. At that time there had been no question of her dying. Now when there is no doubt that the old woman is on her deathbed, she relives the storm in her dreams and recollections. What the experience meant to her only now comes to her awareness. She realizes that she was happy when she was alone in the calm of the storm's eye. She answers the question she has been asking for many years - what is happiness? If she had been allowed, she would have remained in those lustrous moments forever. Happiness is - being protected. A consciousness of nature protects when one realizes that one is part of it. Nature may be violent. Human nature may also be flawed. As sea birds may be at rest, so might she be at peace. The myth of her body disappeared. Death is an evacuation.

In the vagaries of her dream Elizabeth Hunter was aware of her husband. She saw him as her protector, lifting her up, freeing her from the water of the bunker where the debris bumped about her. Then she dreams within a dream. She was at Kudjeri and Alfred was protecting her body with his. There appears to be a tentative conjunction between the protection of man and the protection of nature or God. Both touch her.

The significance of the storm has been realized only afterwards in recollection. The natural person of Elizabeth Hunter became a moral and ethical person. Because White's character was able to make this change, Nature, with its blessings and its flaws, is no longer seen as neutral but purposeful. In pointing out Mrs. Hunter's initial incapacity to conceive man and man in nature as noble, Patrick White is criticizing his character adversely. Thereby he too is no longer neutral. He is demonstrating that Mrs. Hunter was bad and suggesting she is about to be good in spite of her flaws.

LITERATURE AS CRITICISM OF LIFE

When an artist, especially a writer, makes a statement about life, it is almost certainly an assessment. His reflection of life in a particular way from a particular viewpoint at a particular time shows a judgment has been made. The choice of subject, what example to use, is in itself, no matter how existential, an evaluation. The artist does not live in a glass bowl. His audience is bound to ask whether the artist's representation is true or false. Only through hints from the writer of what his conception of honesty is can we learn. When Basil Hunter, at the beginning of this chapter, bounces back with exultation from his night with Florrie and attacks his No-Play, his self-delusion is recognized. The falsity of his life is displayed. On the other hand, when later in this chapter, Mrs. Hunter strums out a showy but shallow piece on the piano and says openly it was the only number she remembered, her honesty is highlighted. In her entire seduction of Pehl, she may have been femininely subtle but one can never judge her as dishonest at this point, not even with herself. Her honesty convinces us of Patrick White's honesty. Later when she asks the nurse for sleeping pills she is on the surface deceptive. Because she knows well that her little lie is not going to succeed, she is shown to be human but not actually dishonest. Patrick White is merely demanding the reader to ask himself why Mrs. Hunter wants to kill herself. To be or not to be has changed Mrs. Lear into a type of Mrs. Hamlet. Was her problem that she no longer felt her life to be important to her children and others? Or was it that her death was more important? Would she have taken the pills if she had been allowed access to them? In the posing of such questions Patrick White's religious concerns are brought to the foreground.

T. S. Eliot in his essay "Religion and Literature" wrote: "The greatness of literature cannot be determined solely by literary standards;..."

DISCIPLINED IMAGINATION

Eliot did not end the above statement with the semi-colon but added, "we must remember [though] that whether it is literature or not can be determined only by literary standards." Patrick White's intention is presented in fictional form and its greatness is achieved through the disciplining of his imagination. The necessity for verisimilitude sets limits. One can imagine a real Mrs. Hunter. For literature's sake she must be important - perhaps even noble. What makes her so is a psychological problem. The assumption that an author "understands" his characters is secondary to the need he has to evoke a response in the reader. That literary skill is required has often been stated but it took Goethe to say, "The best art gives us the illusion of a higher reality." This is in evidence in Patrick White's chapter on the storm.

Mrs. Hunter's participation in the natural event would have been articulated in ancient times as myth. Today Carl Jung's theory of the collective unconscious is available to the artist. Mrs. Hunter preserves unconsciously a universal pattern of the conjunction of man and nature. She is revealed as an archetype. White has prepared us for the elevation by his use of **metaphor** repeated in strength in this chapter.

PRE-STORM

The events, beginning with the helicopter trip to Brumby Island, are described in language prerequisite to the main event. We note that White has diffused and muted his colors: we have coral, shell pink, the tones of tuberoses, faded scarlet (trunks), pale blond (hair), orchids with tufted ears, watery green, blistered green, turquoise blue, white turned golden, feathery clouds, sunset light, moonlight, phosphorescent pubics, sea animals surrounded by luminescent light. This dilution of color accompanies the water and archetypal fish symbolism. Fish and fishing play a role as profuse and sacred in Australian aboriginal folklore as in Judaic-Greco-Christian literature. To early man fish meant food in the coastal regions and inland it meant water, the fertilizer and life-generator. As such the fish continues to be a symbol of the continuance of life and in turn the fisher is the life-seeker and symbol of self-realization. This part of the novel stresses these symbols.

We begin with the crossing of the water by the helicopter. We have the Brumby cottage set near the rolling sea. Slightly inland we have the rain forest and most figuratively we have the sluicing of water from jugs in lieu of plumbing. The Warmings precede the Hunters to the island to get in a little "fishing." The Norwegian Professor Pehl goes fishing, catches fish, and cleans them. Mrs. Hunter cooks and decorates them for the table with wild flowers. The essentials of life are constantly in the forefront of the story. Pehl, as a scientist and modern man, investigates the life of sea animals. They have been named and once named are no longer anonymous. He is able to speak of "benthic segregations." Also White makes use of the fish that ancients named the skiapod. Skiapod, literally from the Greek, means shade foot, shadowy foot. According to mythology there was once a people with such large feet they could use them to shade themselves. A skiapod is also a carnivorous marine animal like a drum fish that can grunt. White's use of it clarifies the fluid relationship between the professor and Mrs. Hunter whose bare feet, like tuberoses, were shadowy and seductive. When Mrs. Hunter spoke of herself to Pehl as a "shadowy fish," her eavesdropping daughter felt like an "electric fish."

The primal qualities of the fish symbolism are doubled in White's food **metaphors** and their sexual overtones. On the island several kitchen scenes are noteworthy. The glamorous Mrs. Hunter peels potatoes while she and her hostess bare their minds on the subject of Scandinavians and French comfort stations, to the disgust of the princess who takes up a paring knife. The scene accentuates the mother's sexuality and the daughter's lack of it. Another kitchen scene is more perverse when the petite Australian wife of a French husband turns out an omelette for the visiting professor. The omelette was too slimy for him. After the fish dinner, when the same professor's face becomes smeared with juice and grease, Mrs. Hunter retreats to the kitchen where she rubs his sunburnt back with lotion. The professor is soothed (seduced?) but the overhearing daughter is provoked into a nearly sleepless night with spasmodic sexual dreams. Next day, beyond the confines of the kitchen and walking in the forest, a relaxed Mrs. Hunter sucks a blade of grass and later when she comes upon the two men felling a tree, she enjoys the compelling taste of a new chip thrown off by the axe. This symbolizes what is to come.

STORM AND AFTERMATH

As White used noun **metaphors** to locate the situation of his characters, on Brumby Island he extends them into action. Instead of nouns to describe noises, sights, smells, contacts, and movements, we have verbs. Metaphoric states of being turn into actions. They not only initiate but activate changes. Water does cleanse and the storm does purge. Mrs. Hunter undergoes a transformation when wind "slams," lightning "tatters," a board "crazes." She "funnels" down the bunker. The bunker door "somersaults." Fireballs "juggle" in the sky. By the time she finds calm in the eye of the storm she has found a new idea about God and death. God was the storm and the storm was testing her. God had prepared her for death. Death would be another test and, having experienced one test, a new one could no longer frighten her. When she knew that the peaceful eye would move along and the storm return, she clawed her way back to the bunker, unafraid.

White uses the cyclone to forecast the storm in the sickroom. We know, however, that no matter what Dorothy and Basil scheme for their mother, the novel is not to be tragic. Mrs. Hunter has already triumphed over despair. The short scene at the chapter's close, when Basil announces the arrangement to put the sick old woman into Thorogood Village, shows the famous actor as a rank amateur. White downgrades him in a series of stutters, alliterativet's and f's.

ARCHETYPAL CRITICISM

There was a time when critics used an author's **metaphors** to decode an author's intentions, even his secrets and private life.

Because White doubles, repeats, and twists his symbols, they are not used to reinforce the meanings being revealed to the reader. The secrets of his characters become challenges to the reader's own intentions, not clues to the author's. This is another facet of the White canon.

THE EYE OF THE STORM

TEXTUAL ANALYSIS

CHAPTER NINE

SYNCOPATION

After the traumatic events described in the last chapter, a return to the straight story of the happenings in the sickroom are welcome reading. Patrick White, as psychologist author, returns us to everyday people and their weaknesses. Even so the content and style are not so simple. In musical terms, White stresses the weak beat. The content is syncopated and the style noisy.

EXORCISM

The cleansing of Mrs. Hunter's soul is repeated in the dance of the housekeeper. The meaning of the dance is twofold. First, Lottie Lipmann wants to relieve herself of the secret that she has fastened her necessity to love someone upon the sick old woman who is her employer. She is compelled to tell her and does it in the only way she knows, in the rhythms of the dance.

Secondly, the dancers become dervishes. Both women are ecstatic. As in the dervish's dance, the chant takes over. While Mrs. Hunter moans, Mrs. Lipmann sings German poetry from the street. Because the dancer knows she no longer believes in the efficacy of her dance and knows the falsity of her song, the **episode** is unbelievably sad. If this scene had been staged in a playhouse, tears would have welled up in many eyes. "Roses never fade; love has them stand up again." Even in this rough translation from the German, the thought is dubious. "You're never going to get lost - you're always newborn." In this sentiment White suggests there rests an ageless truth. At the same time there is no doubt that the reader is being prepared for the death of Elizabeth Hunter, and by hindsight the death of her priestess.

POISON AND AGAIN POISON

An important facet of White's philosophy is drummed and twanged out in this resonant chapter. Because she no longer wanted to be pregnant with Basil Hunter's baby, Florrie had poison on her mind when she went to answer the doorbell. She expected her drug clerk, Col Pardoe, delivering medicine for her patient. She was surprised to find instead Wyburd at the door. He had sprigs of rosemary cupped in his hands. The downbeat comes up. The interchange between the lawyer and the nurse on the subject of the herb, including its use as a stuffing for fish, returns the reader's mind to the previous chapter which White seems to want to keep in prominence directly to the novel's end. The upbeat goes down again when Mrs. Hunter asks Florrie to put her sleeping pills where she can reach them. The **irony** here rests in the fact that Florrie scolds Mrs. Hunter and accuses her for having immoral thoughts such a short time after she had indulged in the same speculations.

PERFIDY OF MAN

The syncopation continues with the **episode** in which Mrs. Hunter dictates a codicil to her will concerning the disposition of her jewelry. Uppink sapphires, down the blue. Double meanings persist in the fact that the old woman is giving Florrie a pink ring to mark her engagement to Col Pardoe who has just been cuckolded by Basil. The downbeat follows the gift of the blue turquoise to Mrs. Wyburd when moments later her husband filches the more expensive sapphire.

The discordant notes sounded in Mrs. Hunter's rasping sarcasm, the muted giggles of the wretched lawyer, and the angry off-side remarks of her nurse are resolved by White at the close when we learn that Sister Mary de Santis is not to receive a jewel. This sister needs no adornment. She is complete in herself. Her dedication to work carries her above a need to possess worldly objects. The **irony** that the sister had worn her new orange hat on her date with Sir Basil is twofold. White gives the reader a choice. Did Mary de Santis resist temptation or was she never given the chance? Does the chapter end with a loud or soft Amen?

THE EYE OF THE STORM

TEXTUAL ANALYSIS

CHAPTER TEN

VARIATION ON A SYMBOL

We can be quite sure that some new sexual insight is to be presented when White introduces the last quarter of the book with an "eating scene." We are moved from the fish of the coast to the mutton of Australian inland.

INCEST

In 1975, over a hundred and fifty years after Byron's death, still another book came off the press attempting to settle once and for all the question of whether or not the poet slept with his sister. If Patrick White is not explicit as to what happened beneath the threadbare blankets of the great Hunter bed, he at least justifies it with considerable psychological acumen. The judges of the Nobel Prize Committee, in making *The Eye of the Storm* their selection, stressed White's strong understanding of the human psyche. The entire form and content of this chapter, which begins the novel's last quarter, leads step after step to the conclusion that incest need not be an abhorrent word.

FROM SINGULAR TO PLURAL

Up to this point Dorothy and Basil have not been portrayed as being lovable or admirable persons. Their main intention has been to get money out of their aged mother so that they might live out their self-admitted pitiful lives in some manner of comfort. They have been cruel, spiteful, and sterile. Any slight hints to the contrary have been minor. So also have been the reasons for the makeup of their psyches. They were the fated children of Alfred and Elizabeth Hunter. Their environment included beginnings on a rough if beautifully located sheep-herding station. They grew up in the turbulence of the growing city of Sydney. Their middle years were spent in the postwar decadence of London and Paris. Throughout their lives each child had toyed with the question, "Who am I?" but it is not until White brings them back to Kudjeri and the question becomes, "Who are we?" that answers are provided.

The drive out to the Macrory station, step one, is more than a bit of narrative. The departure out of the city on the Parramatta Road is described as a sucking back into the past through a "choked intestine." Basil and Dorothy were choked; the traffic of their lives snarled. Step two begins with their stop for food. Nostalgically Basil returns from a shop with two meat pies that are supposed to remind him of his boyhood appetite. Hot, soggy, greasy, gristly, they seem to give some satisfaction to the aging actor. Meanwhile his sister remembers from long ago a traveling salesman in a train. White has again suggested a concurrence of food and sex, the appetites of adolescence. Thereby he raises the proposition that these two appetites are still active. Step three involves their arrival in the fork of the road. In the "cleft" of a surviving stand of trees stands the monument of Alfred Hunter. The statue is a strange representation of a fine gentleman with a fine hand, better suited to resting a book on a fine table. Here it holds the horn of a merino lamb as if the "wrinkles" in his pants might pull him back to earth. Wanting to deny any sexual suggestion either in the statue or in her father, Dorothy urged Basil to drive on. Maliciously Basil shot up the idea that their mother might have included herself in the monument. Basil wanted to be merry but when Dorothy replied that her mother would have put herself on a, "chaise longue," the merriment disappeared. White has clearly introduced here a tie-in between sex hatred and mother hatred.

CONTRASTS IN NORMALCY

Step four accelerates the psychological pattern. Their stay with the Macrorys mirrors their childhood days at Kudjeri. Basil becomes once more a barefoot boy and Dorothy a mother's little helper. Basil literally squelches through mud and gets his foot cut. The burly rancher treats him like a little boy. Dorothy scrubs pots and pans, sews up dresses for the girls, and giggles with them when they stick pins in the dressmaker's dummy Mrs. Hunter had left behind. (The **irony** of the scene is one of the more obvious in the novel.) Meanwhile Rory bares his hairy chest and relaxes before his own fire. Anne (Saint Anne of Kirkaldy) clambers about as best she can. Her pregnancy, regardless of her dusty grey hair, is what would normally be expected.

TRAUMA

The following details might have been extracted from a psychological casebook. The child Basil had been removed from the open spaces of the ranch to the halls and walls of Moreton Drive by a mother who failed to adore dirty little boys who stank of dogs, leather, and the barnyard. When his father came up on occasion to Sydney by train, he took his son to movies which did not appeal. The more exciting big old three-liter Bentley was left in the country. The girl Dorothy too had been removed from the busy kitchen where the boss' ranch hands came to eat their fatty tucker. At her mother's town residence, she took piano lessons from the best teachers. There were maids to answer rings from rooms instead of birds calling from trees. She sat for her portrait with mummy and Basil. Then Basil went away. "I hardly knew my brother."

REGRESSION

The psychology of step five shows the adult at child's play. When his father drove his elegant motor back behind the barn door, his small son had a special pin to dig out the bugs from the radiator. The man remembers. When he once more loiters about in the shadows, Sir Basil tries on a boot too small for his adult foot. He can't get it off. Dorothy, who wanted a little privacy with her brother apart from the ruling Macrorys, discovers him and his predicament. Brother and sister roll on the barn floor in their struggle to free his foot. Between them their efforts bring success. Whereupon Dorothy screams at her brother in words of an uninhibited eight-year-old farm girl. Patrick White has shown us a release from the emotions his character had subconsciously been building up for years. In the drama of the scene there has been no playacting, playwriting, or game playing. No author is reporting. He has disappeared. Marvelously the power of child's play has been revealed.

SIDE-STEPPING

It is too late in the lives of the sophisticated Hunters for them to make progress. The final step which White's psychology has been demonstrating is out of step even if inevitable. What is unusual in childhood can be abnormal in adulthood. It may be natural in both cases. A learning process in childhood may be a disillusion later. In White's metaphoric language and uncannily perceptive rendition of detail, the crawling into bed of Basil and Dorothy seems comfortably valid. They cuddle up in a womb like the twins their mother said they should have been. Masculinity and femininity are two words that never appear. The archetypal Tiresias motif has been brought up to date by a courageous novelist unafraid of truth. White has turned complexes into art.

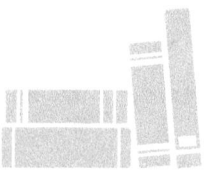

THE EYE OF THE STORM

TEXTUAL ANALYSIS

CHAPTER ELEVEN

PENITENCE

Chapter Eleven begins with a scene which may well be interpreted as confessional. Mrs. Hunter performs an act of contrition in having her tea with Mrs. Wyburd, the woman she betrayed with her husband. Underlying the polite, if ironic, talk and reminiscences of the two old women is the implication that Mrs. Hunter wants to get one last sin out of her system.

THE REAPER

Death is announced in scene two. He appears in various shapes. For this last dance, the predominant colors are symbolically changed to silver and green. Mrs. Hunter's green wig, for once, seems just right. She wears emeralds. The blue sapphire had disappeared. Lottie's top hat and cane are gone too. Instead she drips in slithery sequins and twirls in frothy chiffon - a tunic. Mrs.

Hunter watches her priestess through "a veil of water" which was all her still human vision allowed but knows the dance was entering in the "spirit" of it. She moans and remembers a half dead cow she had come upon as a child. Putrid. She had herself danced then to hide her pity for the beast. Pity is private. All her life she had danced to conceal her pity for those she loved most. She is now loved by the dancer whom suddenly she wants to touch but grabs only the "wind" she creates. The scene continues with a string of words, strung out without grammar, fluid and impressionistic. It concludes on a return from the diaphanous to the reality of pain. Mrs. Hunter wounds her entertainer. As though she knew she must die alone, she dismisses her with a cruel barb and demands the nurse put her on the commode. White is unquestionably asking the reader what Mrs. Hunter wants to relieve herself of.

VICTORY

Poets have killed off their **protagonists** since ages past. The methods of death have varied. Any possibility of a new way seems unthinkable. Yet Patrick White gives a literary presentation for the first time of what must have transpired in fact many times. Dying on a commode is not an innovation. There are records of such in medical annals. On the contrary, what is being called to attention is White's dramatization of the performance of death. Mrs. Hunter performs her death. She is playing "herself" as it was hinted Basil wanted to do in his projected No-play. In contrast to Basil's not too imaginative imitations of Sartre or Beckett, Elizabeth Hunter's act of dying defies comparison. Her lines which begin (page 492) "....I alone must perform whatever the eye is contemplating for me" and ends with "....myself is this endlessness" is a superb statement of White's philosophy on the confluence of the reality of illusion and illusion of reality.

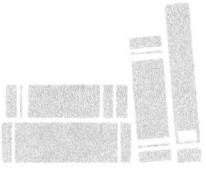

THE EYE OF THE STORM

TEXTUAL ANALYSIS

CHAPTER TWELVE

MEDIATION

The last pages of the book continue with further perceptions concerning the physical and spiritual nature of death. White's metaphors, poetic style, and even humor appear in his summations of the reactions of the characters to the event of Mrs. Hunter's last accomplishment. However, the novel's final curtain does not ring down without an afterglow of love. Life cannot go on for Lottie Lipmann. For the last time her love object had departed. When she opens her veins in the bathtub, symbolically love is being drained out of her. On the other hand, there is the possibility that one dies when there is no more love to drain. In these two alternatives rest the power and meaning of symbolism.

INTRODUCTION TO VOSS

INTERIM NOVEL

When we look at the main line of White's novels from the first big success of *The Aunt's Story* to the prize-winning *The Eye of the Storm*, *Voss* may be perceived as belonging to the same system but only as a spur. It is a much simpler novel and easier to read. The structural plan is straightforward and the characters more clearly delineated. The contrasts are sharp. Though **theme** and style may be associated with earlier and later novels, there are fewer exaggerations and less symbolism. This may be due to the fact that White mulled over this novel over a long period of time. The idea for it, according to White himself in his autobiographical account in *The Prodigal Son*, ("Australian Letters," April 1958) began during his World War II years and persisted regardless of intervening novels until 1957 when *Voss* was published.

Some precedence for White's **theme**, in an over-simplified form, had been dealt with in Ernest Hemingway's *The Old Man and The Sea*. In this novella, manliness was not identified with physical strength or sexual potency but with willpower, pride, and endurance, the chief characteristics of Voss, the explorer.

In a later vein, Joseph Heller's anti-war masterpiece, *Catch-22* followed *Voss* by four years, being published in 1961.

Although Heller's point of view and emphases are quite different from White's, his "artistic statement of man's condition" is comparable. Many similarities in the literary techniques of these authors are obvious, particularly their use of what was called in Heller's time, **Black Humor**. Their use of "patterns of **foreshadowings** and echoes" was highlighted by Walter James Miller in the Monarch Note (00905) on *Catch-22*. Also their use of symbolic "set pieces" is significant. Both men seem to have been influenced by many of the same literary giants of history, namely, Homer, Dante, Shakespeare, Dostoyevsky, Melville, Joyce, and T. S. Eliot. Stylistically, White's earlier uses of paronomasia (punning) and prolepsis are evident in the later novelist.

AUSTRALIA CALLING

Part of the initial interest in *Voss* was that it put a continent on the literary map in a new way. In Australia, Voss contends, "it is possible more easily to discard the inessential and attempt the infinite." The time in which *Voss* takes place, 1848, had been mirrored by other Australian novelists but never with a **protagonist** of *Voss*' bigness or vastness. As in Dante, paradise is glimpsed at the end. The Australian desert becomes the set for all three states, *Inferno*, *Purgatorio*, and *Paradiso*. Voss moves from the inferno of pride, through the purgatory of suffering, to final joy.

As in the *Inferno* we find here murderers, suicides, blasphemers, and others "echoing and **foreshadowing**" the Australian outcasts shipped out from England either justly or unjustly. On the less dark side, we also have a remarkable heroine, Laura, more closely aligned with Petrarch's Laura than Dante's Beatrice. However, in *Petrarch*, Laura dies. In *Voss* Voss dies and Laura survives.

By White's time, the treatment of convict settlers and their richer and better behaved descendants had almost become an unbreakable tradition in Australian novels as had adventures with bush rangers and aborigines. In the manner of Sir Walter Scott, Australian historical novels had seemed attempts at understanding the present through the past. More romantically they followed Byron, particularly in his manly **ballads** of revenge, as in *Mazeppa*.

MAN IN SPACE

In *Voss* White departs from certain Australian "myths" and perhaps becomes more Australian. He makes his explorer, Voss, a German. Here we must remember that White, because of his war experience and his travel in the Rhineland, is particularly knowledgeable on the subject of German psychology. He can use it in fulfillment of his wish to be objective on the subject of Australia. The subject is apart from the object. Voss, the hairy, ungainly, un-English man is "out of" Germany and goes "under" to Australia. Voss learns on the desert that freedom cannot be obtained by flight. From a certain man at a certain time, White drives home for the sake of the people of his homeland a universal truth. Desert barrenness can be helpful.

White lashes out at a hypocritical society early in *Voss*. One of the criticisms implied by White of the Australian elite is that they cannot recognize that an arrogant person, especially a foreigner, may also be sincere and simple. Voss has this dual nature and the reader, if he does not at first recognize it, is taught to sense this and become sympathetic.

The duality within the bounds of one man is repeated in the duality in the space of all Australia. The novel as a whole contrasts the qualities of two kinds of Australian people - those who "huddle along the coast" and those inland bordering the desert. In the character of Laura the two sides of the man and also the two sides of the continent are blended. The movement from the particular to the general, basic in the creation of most good poetry, is handled spatially by White. *Voss* is a novel that may be compared to a piece of sculpture, rather than a portrait of a man, because it moves around in space.

DEVIL AND SUPERMAN

Voss plays Mephisto. He is the ubermensch or superman. He is Milton's Satan who carries his own devil within him. To will is the answer to what. He sees himself as God. For this reason he appears to Judd, one of the men on the expedition, as the Devil. Such a figure is usually avoided by modern writers of realistic fiction. They seem to lack White's audacity to produce a man in the tradition of Melville's *Captain Ahab*. Voss, like most Germans in English literature, superficially lacks humor. He is also a skeptic, meaning he sees the other side, which is part of humor. Sadly enough, skepticism, like humor, can turn within; thereby turning the humorist into victim. As a consequence Voss is both comic and tragic and so, in a fashion, satisfies the post-World War II demand that there should be something absurd about a hero. To rise to heights he must be humiliated. Unlike Ahab, who goes down with distinction, Voss is humbled. He gains grandeur only in death. In Voss' dying White utilizes a typical Australian aboriginal idea - the concept of the migration of spirit. At death the soul goes into another body. As we shall see from several of the aboriginal passages in the book, the soul flies upward and outward like birds or kites. So Voss' journey into the hinterland spreads a goodness over Australia after the man is dead.

TO THE WILDERNESS

As Christ moved to the wilderness, so Voss struggles in the desert where all worldly things become unimportant. In seeing the link, we are made aware of the paradox of Man in Christ and Christ in Man. It is this paradox that White tried to witness and solve to some degree in each of his earlier novels. Voss' journey is both an allegory of the progress of the human soul towards God and also a vision of what it is striving for. Voss' megalomania at the outset verges on blasphemy. The best part of Voss is Laura who pulls him back when vast distances separate them. Both Laura and Voss are rationalists. They are also religious skeptics but not atheists like Le Mesurier, the thinker of the expedition who cuts his own throat when hope runs out.

TRIANGLES

Le Mesurier stands on one side of the Christ figure of Voss. On the other is Harry Robarts (not quite robot but art robber or artful thief) who is a kind of innocent boy-fool who falls in love with his image of Voss. White's use of the "fool in literature" is always original.

In another typical variation, Voss is not the son of a carpenter but the son of a timber merchant. This subtly humanizes the narration which sustains another triangular relationship between the characters. Central is Judd, the ex-convict, who was forced on Voss by one of the expedition's sponsors. He is the only one in the entire group who is not weaker than Voss. He is flanked on one side by Turner (who turns coat), a crude and sensuous natural man. On the other side is Angus, a rich rancher, a gentleman, who joined up out of weakness. Between the two sets of trios is Palfreyman, the botanist, the go-between. White's choice of this name enlightens the reader. A palfrey is a saddle horse for everyday riding. In no sense is he a war horse or a work horse. He is a runaway from the dramas of the everyday world and yet this collector of butterflies and small flowers is one of the first to discover the changes in Voss. He says, "I must condemn the morality and love the man." This is not the conclusion reached by the other odd man out, Jackie, the aboriginal boy who becomes the executioner. On the other hand it is possible to conceive Jackie as a mercy killer.

JOURNEY TO HELL 'N' BACK

Such is the narrative. As such it is full of treachery, violence, and surprises. It is also a story of what events do to men, even superior men. It is also a story of what people do to people. But it is not a tragedy. Voss' pride is altered by Laura and his quest is successful. The story is continued beyond Voss' death. It is a divine comedy because the vision is fulfilled. The base metal of Voss is purified. Laura knows that when a man is humbled he may ascend.

VOSS

TEXTUAL ANALYSIS

CHAPTERS 1-5: UP TO THE DEPARTURE

POWER OF WILL

Voss believed that one can make his own future. Willpower makes things come about. The Greeks recognized that such a concept is not unnatural in men. They also believed that the will of man could also be in conflict with the will of the gods and that only an arrogant man challenges the gods. Voss is an arrogant man. Pride damns him in this highly charged story. In contrast to the novel Patrick White was to write twenty years later, *The Eye of the Storm*, in which a very old woman succeeds in willing herself to die, Voss is a loser. He is killed by the power of nature, not by the power of will. The Australian desert he was determined to conquer overcomes him. It would seem that White, in the interval between *Voss* and *The Eye of the Storm*, had reversed himself. Not so, because what makes a man tick is not buried with him. If old Mrs. Hunter's death represents a purging for a maturing Australia, then Voss' death is not an end but a beginning. The novel concerns Australia in its seed time. Voss may be likened to a proud, boastful Prometheus, the god who brought man the gift of fire. Voss put a spark under Australia that White makes us feel is not about to go out.

LESS THAN HONEST

Voss is a man and like most men, he sometimes gets mixed up in his philosophy. He despises humility and deprives whatever god he believes in of any such quality. His god is above humility. Voss tries to be honest. He thinks of himself as a logical thinker and is pleased when he meets a young woman who thinks the way he does. Yet the man is dishonest when he tells himself he does not need a beautiful woman. He refuses to be seduced by the turn of a lovely neck. In the opening scene White clothes her in a deep blue dress which is, to be sure, symbolically virginal. On the other hand, when we read about the rustling of her petticoats beneath the blue, the author's intent seems tentative. Is White also being less than honest? Deliberately so in these first pages? We have already learned that Laura twisted the truth when she begged off going to church because of a headache. She had indeed remained at home because she was afraid she might be "suffocated by the fuzz of faith." The alliterative f's are not accidents in the presentation of the fuzziness of Voss' and Laura's philosophy. At the same time an honest reader is warned to keep an open mind.

CONTRASTS IN HONESTY

On the return from church of the Bonner family we seem to get a picture of healthy bustling honesty. In White fashion the picture so set up begins to fade almost at once and continues until we see Mr. Bonner as a forerunner of a late twentieth-century wheeler-dealer. Going to church was convenient to his position as prosperous merchant and downtown man of respectability. Not unlike Moses, the pillar of his religion becomes his pillow. He organized Voss' expedition because it would be good for Australia. And perhaps his business? To give the expedition the tone that this German lacks he places under his charge Palfreyman whose ornithological researches were being sponsored by a British peer. Also he was happy to see Angus of Dulverton sign up. Mr. Bonner likes to do good. He hires ex-convicts - cheap. Such a person is Rose, one of the housemaids. Pregnant, she shall grow in importance as well as size. But Mr. Bonner did not hire her until she had been emancipated. He took no chances until her honesty had been guaranteed by someone else.

BOYISH AUSTRALIA

White brightens up his picture of Bonner by showing how boyish he is. He has a love of conspiracy that becomes apparent in his arrangements for the cavalcade. He even seems to conspire with Voss. It is ironic that here the little boy who writes his name in blood and swears to persist is Voss and not Bonner who dies in his own bed. Youthful too is the figure of the scarlet-coated Lieutenant Radclyffe, his future son-in-law who would also come into his own financial success. White treats this young blade more benevolently especially as a later generation Australian, not quite so boyish. Ideas might disturb Radclyffe's brains and his manliness if he were to read books. He is contrasted with Voss to whom he is arrogantly rude. In the German tradition, Voss has many ideas, even **metaphysical** ones. With him the exercise of intellect is not a feminine but a masculine characteristic. He sees the lieutenant's dashing uniform as a mere cover for a soft and stupid interior. The old world Teuton makes no allowances for youth. It is with characteristic twists that White makes the European intolerant of the old world figure governing the Australian colonists. White turns his acidic **satire** upon his excellency, the governor, who fails to show up at the wharf to celebrate the expedition's departure. His lordship sent his colonel who speechifies on the subjects of farewells, safe returns, the union jack, and the "illustrious Queen." There is still another twist in the fact that the blows of White's sallies against the English and their non-intellectual dependents are softened by none other than the German Voss. It was Voss who stood up for Australia in whose vastness he saw greatness.

MODERN TYPES

As we were able to recognize a modern opportunist in White's portrait of Bonner, we can see a "drop-out" in Frank Le Mesurier. The paronomasia on Frank, frank, and Le Mesurier, the evaluator, is informative. Frank's desire to be frank with himself as he assesses the world around him with all its inconsistencies makes him ineffectual. He is always about to do something worthwhile, something to approximate beauty. He is a would-be poet, and a snob, bored by the less brainy and the less honest. He has a counterpart in another member of the group, the hard-hat Turner whose tough qualities and cunning craftiness Voss sees as assets. In revealing these characters White seems to be challenging the reader to draw conclusions he may have to abandon.

FEMALE INTUITION

Four women play roles in the action of the opening scenes. Laura, whose strong will matches Voss' at their first meeting, acts as his protector at the picnic where Voss is surrounded by the men of Bonner's acquaintance. On the wharf for the departure, her will is displayed again when her horse shies and she controls it. Here her firm hands are supplementary. She had been slightly dishonest when she used Palfreyman to learn more about Voss. Her female intuition tells her Voss is a lost man. Mrs. Bonner has already exhibited the same feeling when she doubted her husband's selection of Voss as leader. She called the German a "scarecrow," already lost. Her daughter, Belle, whose creamy vapidity seems interested only in widening her acquaintance with those who received invitations to Governor's balls, also displays some haunting fears. When she watches a pair of aborigine women, in scanty shifts, preparing their simple meal regardless of the fashionable folk gathered for the send-off, she intuitively wishes she was free of society's situations. Rose, the maid who faints not from hard work but from her "condition," is highly intuitive. All heart, she is White's forerunner of Lottie Lipmann in *The Eye of the Storm*. In Rose's past she killed her child and not herself as Lottie did. She had taken the babe's life because she loved it. Nevertheless the world called her a monster and deported her. We are forced to wonder what will result from this second pregnancy. White is demonstrating that suspense may be interwoven with character analysis.

WAYS OF KNOWING

Closely allied to female intuition is the sensitivity of Harry Robarts (similar to but not equal to Robot). In the tradition of literature's wise fool, he is more than an "easy shadow to wear." White, however, varies the tradition because Harry's way of knowing is not the result of his wit. He does not understand but senses. He is aware of the feminine streak in Palfreyman. He feels drawn to him but then almost immediately feels guilty. He must remain loyal to Voss, his first friend. In his premonition that Palfreyman is shameless in his humility and in his openly confessed need for God's help, the boy Harry sees clearly that it would be Palfreyman who would "melt or turn to ashes." White is preparing us for another of the novel's psychological spirals. Harry's sensitivity, later to be reflected in the similar canniness of the aborigines, is projected against the hard shell of the Bonner class.

METAPHORIC TEACHING

White's metaphors, early in the book, are highly informative. The **metaphor** of the widening circle is typical. It is Voss who watches the still water disturbed by a pebble. He allows his thoughts "to widen on it." Equally provocative are the developing figures of kites and birds. Laura, who had given up praying, was to begin again. She would send out her prayers, as though written on bits of paper that would wing their way to Voss as he led the expedition. They forecast the letter of Voss to Laura that the aborigines were to scatter to the winds. They were relieving themselves of the white man's curses scratched like bird tracks, in crazy lines of ink. Also prophetic is the happening when the Governor's colonel has made his farewell speech, as it were from the horse's mouth; a horse lets its droppings perfume the assemblage.

ARCHETYPAL JOURNEY

Voss' expedition into Australia is both physically and psychologically in the tradition of the journey motif. The novel has been compared to the travels of Odysseus. Because Voss' account does not begin in the middle, in medias res, as does Homer's **epic**, the story of Telemachus is forgotten. White's **protagonist** is both father and son. If Bonner fathers the expedition, then Voss is the son. But Voss is also the father to each of the members. He is also the son who was compelled to wrest his freedom from his German parents. His Australian venture is thereby coupled to the archetypal initiation motif of Odysseus' son, Telemachus. At the end of the book the White spiral is again revolved upward when the bronze figure of Voss is raised to memorialize him as a father of Australia. These two motifs may be observed wandering in and out of the main story line.

GREEK PHILOSOPHY

Voss said that atheists are apt to be atheists for the wrong reasons. They abandon God because they make him in their own image. The Greeks too anthropomorphized their gods. With the Greeks man was good and it was man's duty to strive to be beautiful, to be an ideal man. But the atheist, to Voss, sees man as evil. His god in whose image he is made must also be evil and accordingly not worth believing in. The Greeks were in opposition to the Old Testament statement that God made man in His own image, whereby man is God-like. Voss swings between these two positions. He looks down upon Palfreyman who seems to wear his religion on his sleeve. Yet, at the book's end Voss is forced to admire the man for his courage. A change has simultaneously occurred in Voss' philosophy. To be truly courageous, particularly at the moment of death, one must have learned to be humble. This change is the result of a process, a processional in the book's journey motif.

SET SCENES

White's propensity for staging big set scenes has already been demonstrated in this early novel. The Pringle picnic at Point Piper was played before a massive proscenium on more than one level - from the upper grounds, where the carriages were unloaded, down to the rocks at the water's edge. So at the top we found White's surface details of the occasion. We were aware of ubiquitous children and attendant coachmen doubling as outdoor butlers. Chops broiled over hot coals, lips blew over steaming tea, thin sandwiches were nibbled, and elders were uncomfortable on carpet stools. Lower down, Laura and Voss were bumping each other on the rocks of getting to know each other. White's symbolic tricks are obvious. However, the **metaphors** are fewer than those of his later big pieces. Food is not yet so closely tied to sex. The humor is gentler; the comedy is more subtle. The **satire** lacks the bite of the description of dinner parties of *The Eye of the Storm*. By comparison the picnic is more indicative of child's play.

SENSE AND SENSIBILITY

The nature of the picnic approaches the lady-like qualities of Laura's Sunday morning reception of Voss. It is suggestive of Jane Austen's brilliance in similar scenes. The variations White was later to make on Austen's sensibility, notably in *The Vivisector* (1970), are here still tentative. When Voss could not go on with the reading of the poem that Mrs. Bonner unfeelingly selected for him, sensibility is less obvious than sensitivity. White's heroes do not yet have the control over their feelings that Austen's do. Voss' private emotions explode, senselessly. This boiling over of inner intensity (already noted in Harry Robarts) is soon to be echoed in the aborigine boy Jackie, whom we meet in the next section.

VOSS

TEXTUAL ANALYSIS

CHAPTERS 6-13: THE APPROACHES TO HELL

PLOT TO DOUBLE PLOT

The diversification of scene already mentioned in the first section is accentuated in this one by the complete alternation of terrain by whole chapters. The blue bush, the fragrant scents, and the exotic birds of the inland reflect the pace of action as much as the roses, the laurels, and the shining shrubs of coastal civilization. White uses variation in nature as springboards to advance not only his surface story but also his underlying themes. When we learn that the aborigines placed their dead on tree platforms not merely to get them off the ground, but so that their spirits might depart more easily, like birds, we are getting an insight into White's philosophy concerning the rational and the irrational, the physical and the spiritual. In similar vein, when Laura suggests pear blossoms for Belle's bridal bouquet, the black sticks which bear the fragile flowers are telling us not only that black sticks may occur in Belle's marriage but that all life is transitory. Like the alternations of blossoms, fruit, and black sticks, White keeps his two plots moving. In each stage they are different but in each the philosophy is the same, confirmed in both.

THEMATIC STATEMENT

Oddly enough one of the novel's primary **themes** is not repeated by Voss but by Frank Le Mesurier. White does this deliberately but only after the reader's feeling toward these two characters has undergone a change. Frank, the drifter, has come into his own. He talks to Voss, who, under the influence of the peaceful first days of the expedition, has drawn out the young man's past. Voss had done this with each man in a way that advances the humanity of everyone concerned. That these serious confidences also foreshadow the troubles ahead is secondary to the composite statement. When Frank says that the mystery of life is not solved by success, the implication runs deep. The author is making a statement. Voss, the perpetual seeker, is being compared with the likes of the Bonners who are always more or less blinded by success. The lesson here is that failure is a learning vehicle. Achievement is less important than the struggle for it. Voss' effort, the Odysseus idea, teaches this. Voss, after he fails but before he dies, learns and teaches what gives meaning to life. It is an extraordinary bit of White's **irony** that the reasons for living come from the man who commits suicide. Yet in this very **irony** a tangent truth may be suggested. Having lived variously, having become a partner in humanity, Frank, still a loner, desires to have a new experience. He wants to create something new which would never be possible because of his sick and wasted body. There is nothing more he can do in this life so he seeks one beyond. This philosophy is a predecessor to that stated by old Mrs. Hunter in *The Eye of the Storm*.

AUSTRALIAN ANTITHESIS

White's comparison of Rhine Towers and Jildra serves as a qualitative analysis of Australian society. The cavalcade's first long stop after leaving the coast is at Rhine Towers, the well-run and prosperous station of Mr. Sanderson. This spot, set on hilltop rocks, bronze and golden at sunset, reminded Voss of his homeland's castles. Equally German in its feeling was the cleanliness and attentiveness of Mrs. Sanderson. The table she put forth was bounteous. Her linen was immaculate. Voss was so impressed he was inclined to think the luxury was weakening had it not been so well deserved through hard work. Unfortunately the pure gold of the place gradually turned yellow. First by the introduction of the two men who came to join the expedition. Judd is an ex-convict, chosen by Sanderson because of his familiarity with the bush, and secondly there is Angus Dulverton, the young gentleman rancher. Unsuspectingly, Mrs. Sanderson placed them side by side at the dinner table where Angus' displeasure at sitting next to the freed man tarnished the meal with prejudice. This is followed by Mrs. Sanderson's going-to-bed comment to her husband about Voss' sallowness. (Palfreyman had already fainted with sickness.) She is fearful for the expedition. She worries about Voss' ability to endure. White is preparing his readers.

Antithetical to the health and prosperity of Rhine Towers is Jildra, the next and last station where supplies were to be provided. The place is a **parody** on the best of Australia as exemplified by the Sandersons. Brendan Boyle (brendan, burning up, and boil) is allowing his settlement to putrefy. His slovenliness disgusts Voss. Drinking too much, indulging his sex upon giggling aborigine women whose red-headed children attest to his incontinence, Boyle exists from day to day with no thought for the morrow. He is sour on life and releases his daemons from a filthy mouth. His obsessions were not born out of ignorance. They compare unfavorably to the superstitions of the black men who, here confined within the bounds of Jildra, are also a dirty lot.

AUSTRALIAN ABORIGINES

In this section White demonstrates how sympathetically he feels toward the Australian aborigines. We are introduced to Jackie, the black boy whose fate is joined with Voss'. He is unclad but for a bit of something almost the color of his skin. He is shameless but shy. He is sensitive to the good vibrations coming from Voss. He is delighted with the present of a jackknife. (There is no thought that it might become a murder weapon.) He is a grateful boy, devoted immediately to his leader. Jackie is flanked by Dugald, the grey-haired aborigine whose sense of fun is typified by the tatters of a black swallowtail coat he is wearing. To his joy the coat has a pocket sewn into one tail that flaps around his bare buttocks. White's appreciation of the delightful childishness of Dugald is a forerunner of the comic scene when the native women, having been given a sack of white flour, throw it all over themselves and others as though they were English youngsters playing in the season's first snow. Here White seems even a bit envious of the aboriginal way of life.

LOW KEY PATHOS

What the aborigine people did for the fun of it made the white men realize how long it had been since they had been able to be childishly happy. The whorls of tossed flour reminded them of Christmases in England. With the best of intentions

Voss decided his men needed a respite from their travels. The 24th of December was, he guessed, a good time for it. In what might have been one of White's best set pieces, the comedy turns black. Instead of carols on Christmas eve, they listened to a howling set up by their dogs. Even though Dugald was sick, probably from fear and superstition, Voss took him and Jackie to find the cause of the dog's alarm. The men still at camp heard Voss' shots and learned next morning that half their cattle had been driven off. Nevertheless, in an attempt to ignore the tragedy, Palfreyman reads the appropriate Christmas lessons from the prayer book. Harry gets them to sing "God Save the Queen." Judd cooks mutton regardless of the flies above and the maggots beneath.

It would appear that White was treating us to an exercise in pathos had it not been for the appearance of the aborigines themselves. Their women were naked. Their hair had been plucked even in the most secret places. The white men laughed and the black men hissed. White has given us a lesson in perversion and innocence.

BLACK MAGIC

There is, however, in this section a truly magnificent "set comic piece" that is enjoyable. It contrasts so sharply with the Christmas celebration that we are impressed with the breadth of White's vision. The scene is set in the cave Voss and Jackie had stumbled upon when they were searching for protection from the rains that followed the scorching drought. Down into the cave through a strange break in a shaft an eerie light filtered. Bats screamed about. But Jackie was delighted with it as a possible haven. He saw only good magic in the human bones and blowing feathers. The men were all dead; only their spirits flew about like birds, unseen. Since no harm would come, Voss and Jackie persuaded their followers to move in, taking special care of Frank, too sick to stir on his own. Once within, they relaxed. They became aware of the cave drawings on the walls. Figures of snakes and kangaroos offered a new interest. Best of all were the female representations. The weary men forgot their troubles in jokes. Laughter had a medicinal effect - a bit of relief White seems to feel his readers would also enjoy.

THOUGHT TRANSFERENCE

Along with his variations in tempo with the progress of the deteriorating expedition, White whisks us back and forth to the events taking place in the Bonner mansion. He does this with the old literary trick of letter writing, already mentioned in the analysis of *The Eye of the Storm*, see page 17. Here again White interjects a variation into the traditional mode. It is noteworthy that letters written and received are presented to us by the recipient. Letters destined to be lost are presented at the time of the letter writing. There are two of each. Still White's variation is not complete because, regardless of whether the letter is received or not its message gets through. Voss receives the knowledge of the love Laura has for him and Laura senses all that was important for Voss. This is even true of the letter Laura tore up and did not send. Such thought transference is expanded by White to include a measure of ESP (extra-sensory perception). For example, Rose, when walking in the garden with Laura, who has Voss uppermost in her thoughts, predicts the arrival of his letter. As a matter of fact it had already been delivered to Mr. Bonner's office. He turns it over to Laura that same evening.

CREDULITY QUOTIENT

Very different is White's handling of Laura's obsession concerning Rose's expected baby. Mr. Bonner calls it her "unhealthy imagination." Although White's readers would probably agree with this, it is nevertheless the author's intention that Laura's trouble may be a natural one and accordingly understandable. She is very, very much in love with Voss, even greedily so, yet knows that all signs have pointed to the improbability of their union. They have been so spiritually close that a physical reaction was inevitable though miles separated them. Rose, her maid and constant companion, is pregnant. How easy for Laura in her passion, sorrow, and longing to imagine a baby's kick within her own body. When on her deathbed Rose names her baby girl "Mercy." She seems to be saying, "take her, have mercy on Laura." Because of this the reader is asked to understand Laura's refusal to allow Mrs. Bonner to remove the illegitimate child to a more suitable home. Without stretching plausibility, White is illustrating the expanding power of love.

THEATRICAL ELEVATION

Less acceptable may be some of Laura's day-dreams. Yet her almost transcendental feelings, especially her experience at the cemetery when Rose is being lowered into the grave, is not so unusual as to be out of bounds. At such a time the limitations of space and time often do seem to disappear.

Along with Laura's sensation of riding along with Voss on his journey, we can appreciate Voss' hallucination of Laura's smile when in fact it is Judd who is binding up his wound. Starvation has often been known to stimulate imagination.

One bit of lunacy in the story is saved not only because of its universality but because of White's literary and dramatic genius. This is the sleep-walking **episode**. By a trick of moonlight, Palfreyman, who is watching Voss walk, thinks he sees Voss' hand detach itself. The next morning the prismatic compass has disappeared and we immediately think of Shakespeare's Lady Macbeth. Then when White tells us the compass was returned to its rightful place and Voss admits no knowledge of its disappearance or replacement, the reader is kept guessing. The **episode** is a **foreshadowing** of the disaster accompanying the second loss of the compass. The compass is used by White as a symbol for finding direction with spiritual as well as physical connotations. The symbolism is doubled when finally the compass is washed away by the waters of the flooding river.

RESURRECTION SYMBOL

Of the many symbols and **metaphors** used, one of the most outstanding is the utilization of the resurrection symbol. Once more White revitalizes it to further his **theme**. Because of a typical White twist, we do not really know whether Voss or Palfreyman represents the living Christ. Recalling that Voss orders Palfreyman to go forward to deal with the hostile rabble of aborigines, we may feel that Palfreyman is the chosen one. As the blacks stood their ground like trees (the crucifixion), Palfreyman goes forward, unarmed. As he himself avers, he needs none. "I will trust in my faith." The character who has been weak up to this point has become miraculously strong. When Palfreyman is speared to death, Judd fires his gun. A black tumbles and fumbles with his guts. The tribe flees. Palfreyman was the savior. The symbolism is extended when at the hasty burial of Palfreyman, Harry Robarts sees a white bird 'ascend" from the grave. Harry's thought or imagination had, ironically, been engendered by Harry's contact with the black boy Jackie whose aboriginal concept of the incarnation of the spirits is no longer new to the reader. The **irony** of the "savior" symbolism is again extended by White. Later, Voss, alone because of death or abandonment, is finally stabbed to death by Jackie, his black protege who performs the act with his jackknife. Voss' "ascent" is less spiritual than Palfreyman's white bird but as we see in the novel's last section, it will be perhaps the more enduring.

SNAKE COMET

The short period between Palfreyman's and Voss' deaths is dramatized by the appearance of the comet. If it was White's intent to offer Voss as a betrayer of Palfreyman, a Christ figure, and then to develop Voss' death as a sacrifice for the mankind of Australia, the snake provides the poetic, perhaps even the **epic** twist. Comets have been used as prophetic omens by the earliest bards. Shakespeare, who may have witnessed a dramatic performance of the natural phenomenon in his own time, used them in more than one play.* For the Australian black man the comet is the big white father of heaven. He can be either good or bad. In this case the aborigines feel his appearance is the result of his anger. A white man has shot and killed one of their tribe and he has not been avenged. To be sure Le Mesurier is dead, killed not by the blacks but by his own hand. The one remaining white man, though he be dying, must be the victim. So it transpires that Voss loses his life to satisfy a demanding god. Here the snake comet god is bad. But is he? White seems to be asking the question mankind seems never to give up asking. How can God do such terrible things to his people, even innocents, and still be considered a loving God, a good God? In this novel the answer is provided by Laura, as she lies sick with fever in the Bonner home. When at dawn Mrs. Bonner is startled up from her chair in Laura's room where she had been keeping watch, she was frightened by her niece's crying out, "It is over. It is over." To the older women the cry is a sign Laura's fever had broken and she thanks God. To Laura, the vision in her dream had told her Voss' agony was over. He was dead. At about the same time Mrs. Bonner draws the curtains and sees the comet. It is a beautiful sight - so beautiful she wants Laura to see it too. But Laura says she has already seen it. The sparkling symbol of the comet had moved from Voss' desert to show itself in all its glory to loved ones in Sydney. The snake comet god is good.

HERMENEUTICS

The science or art of hermeneutics which in years past was largely confined to the study and interpretation of biblical scripture has more recently developed into the study and analysis of myths, their origins and relationships. Leading hermeneuticists have been able to relate their work to the psychologist, Carl Jung, who has already been mentioned in this guide. Patrick White's awareness of the relatedness of various myths appears in almost all of his work. His use of dreams and dream psychology just referred to in Laura's vision of Voss' death is an indication, and there are others in other novels - his familiarity with the myth of Vishnu, the sleeping god; the myth of Isis and Osiris, the dying and resurrected god; the myth of Prometheus, the defier, thrown out of heaven, the bringer of fire to men, also the unkillable; the myth of nativity appearing in many religions, the feathered serpent Quetzalcoatl was born of a virgin - these and others are used in White's interpretations of contemporary man. By expressing himself in the extended myths of symbols, metaphors, and other poetic figures, White's individual men and women become universal.

* e.g., "As stars with trains of fire and dews of blood, " *Hamlet*, Act 1: Scene 1.

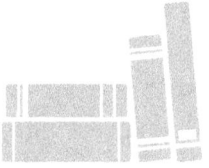

VOSS

TEXTUAL ANALYSIS

CHAPTERS 14-16: THE AFTERGLOW

SYDNEYSIDERS

Although White has a certain admiration for the swagger of Australian society, his **satire** can be extremely knifelike. We have already felt the venom of his comparison of the mercantile rich, as typified by the Bonners, to their former slaves, the workhouse convicts, such as the pregnant Rose, and the black natives. In this last section we have a satiric **parody** of Voss in the later day explorer, Colonel Hibden, the dominant figure at the scene of the unveiling of the bronze statue of Voss. Hibden lacks Voss' altruism. He went to the hinterland to learn more of the fate of Voss and his men. Contrary to Voss, he succeeds in making a return. He brings a few facts but no real information of lasting value. He uses Voss, his predecessor, to make a big show for himself in front of the Australian officials and foreign dignitaries. White cuts him down to size.

LOOSE ENDS

White also uses the commemorative scene to tie up some of the novel's loose ends in his presentation of the attending guests. Introducing Bell Bonner without her husband, Radclyffe, we can see that the Bonners of the next generation have not moved forward. From White's viewpoint they augur little for the good of Australia. John and Rose Marie Beston in their essay "Spiritual Progression in Voss" call attention to the fact that Frank Le Mesurier, in his notebooks read by Voss, prophesied the statue ceremony. "After persecution and humiliation," Mr. and Mrs. Beston write, "comes public honor which is only an externalization of the exalted state of the soul." They then quote White in Frank's notebook, "They chase this Kangaroo, and when they have cut off his pride, and gnawed his charred bones, they honor him in ochre on a wall." The Bestons then continue on their own, "That is true not only of Old Man Kangaroo among the aboriginals but Christ among the Christians, and of Voss among the people of Sydney at the Domain ceremony. The spirit of Old Man Kangaroo, of Christ, and of Voss has gone out, it has gone away, it is everywhere in a dissolution that is supreme fulfillment."

The point is strengthened by none other than Judd, now a mentally deteriorating old man who is at the unveiling. He tells Laura that the aborigines continue to talk of Voss. Voss is more than a legend to them as he is to Laura who also feels in spite of herself that Voss is "still out there."

AUTHOR'S SUMMATION

White's ability to concentrate on one man's value to his own and later generations is vexingly noteworthy. He compels the reader to admit, regardless of his own sympathy toward his hero, that Voss did not further communication within the different strata of Australian society. (This is a subject more fully treated by White in subsequent novels.) This failure, which may have autobiographical undertones on White's part, is hinged to the reversal of roles between Voss and Laura. From the novel's first chapters we were offered the impression that Voss is an idealist but ineffectual whereas Laura was more sympathetic to the materialism of her prosperous relatives. After his death, it is Voss and his ideals that endure. Laura, who had once caused the Bonner world to quake, seems in the long run less influential. She continues to live in Sydney where she is an intelligent and courageous mistress of a girls' school - a disappointment to herself and to the reader.

Voss, as one of White's most unorthodox personalities, may have failed but he is not a disappointment. He failed to overcome the Australian bush. He did not fail to overcome his own nature. He may have failed in his answers to philosophical and religious questions but he is justified. His spirit persists.

In another article, "Alienation and Humanization, Damnation, and Salvation in Voss," Mr. Beston writes: "Greater stress is placed upon the contrast between Voss' constant striving to learn human reactions and Laura's denial of human emotions." To quote further from this same note, "To White, damnation is the preservation of an individual's isolation from mankind while salvation is the abandonment of one's notion of special separateness."

ON DISAGREEING WITH PATRICK WHITE

Some critics, mostly Australians, have contended that some of White's philosophical assertions have been false. They object to his transposition into other worldliness. To these reviewers the reality of illusion is not acceptable. From the opposite viewpoint, a few quotations from the dramatist, Eugene Ionesco, writing in *The London Times Literary Supplement*, Oct. 6, 1972, are relevant. Ionesco was discussing what he called "the play of passions" in the work of Pirandello and Brecht. His remarks support White's aims and achievements. They include: "A work of art is a monument which is neither false nor true but dwells on a different plane from that of truth or falsehood. The work of art is real, it finds its reality in the imaginary world...it is sincerity and existence.... Philosophers and theorists may be wrong in the abstract generality of their interpretations; art cannot be wrong, it is representative, it is the expression of our truth in an actuality renewed by emotion.... An artist cannot lie because he is not trying to mislead - that is to say, he is not trying to be anyone but himself, because his essential vocation is to express himself, to be the way he is, to testify to what he sees, hears and records."

THE AUNT'S STORY

THE SOLITARY

This novel, first published in 1948, received complimentary reviews in England and America, if not in Australia. It brought its author to the forefront among professional novelists . In it White had found a character of the type congenial to his style and philosophy, one that he has never forsaken. Theodora Goodman abides in one form or other, if always in different settings, within all of White's heroes and heroines who later come to life. As she was the first, so Theodora is the loneliest of them all - so also did she herald White's **theme** that no one can escape one's aloneness. There is always a part of every one of us that defies communication. Theodora, the spinster of the tawny skin and black hat, with its floppy rose, is the most extraordinary of White's protagonists. An ordinary human being who was not born crazy, she develops gradually and realistically into a schizophrenic. Since she is not idealized or romanticized, she can make readers uncomfortable. Yet they will be rewarded. This is the way one of the first reviewers expressed it in *The New York Herald Tribune Book Review*: "This exceedingly brilliant and likeable novel is written with an almost miraculous liveliness. It ripples with gaiety and a razor-edged love of life."

WHITE AS CHILD PSYCHOLOGIST

White's portraits of children have been criticized as being records of child types rather than individuals. Actually but a few children appear in his novels. When they do, they are important only as indicators of adults they are to become. In this sense White's understanding is psychologically sound, particularly in this novel where the child is (apologies to Wordsworth) mother to the woman.

Theodora is barren, consequently she is flawed and desires freedom from her imprisonment. She is unable to compensate by assuming motherhood as Laura Trevelyan was to do later in *Voss*. In still another sense she anticipates a character in *Voss*. She is a feminine forerunner of Frank Le Mesurier whom we have dubbed a "drop out." The switch from the female Theodora to the male Frank also bears out White's understanding of the bisexuality of the Tiresias myth.

As a child in the yellow house amid the black hills, Theodora had witnessed the sexual act of a poor servant girl. Her childhood shock keeps her running throughout the rest of her life. She is always "about to." She is not an artist. She cannot produce anything tangible, as Frank was finally able to do.

Ironically she is nevertheless spiritually fertile. She is the first of White's illuminati. She is able to see, as Blake put it, "the infinite in everything." This ability is both a blessing and a curse. It extends her capacity for humility. She is always learning to be humble (Voss did not begin until he was close to death). She dreams of perfect humility. This creates the tension in her strong personality that eventually leads to her disintegration. She is destroyed by her own mind as Voss was later to be destroyed by the forest of nature.

WAR'S LEFTOVERS

Theodora is continually searching for the way to find her own holy grail. She comes closest to it in Italy. The Hotel du Midi with its "jardin exotique" is a temporary Eden. In this microcosm of Europe after the war, "where the rich gather to admit their poverty," the emigres are the European Bonners of former times. They have been transformed by war and the personal losses it brought. Theodora suffers with them and touches their souls. However, since no **protagonist** of White's can be a sentimentalist, Theodora sees them for what they are. There is the Russian general, Sokolnikov, who was not a general but a liar and cheat. Yet he is saintly and reminiscent of Dostoyevsky's Alyosha in *The Brothers Karamazov*; equally well-portrayed is Katina, the unwanted child, and Mrs. Rapallo who puts on a good front.

As Voss was burnt up in the desert by the ravages of fever, so Theodora was exhausted by her "love" for these people. Finally there was an actual conflagration. Fire destroyed the Hotel du Midi in a big scene such as White was to develop later in set pieces. At this point White's characteristic sense of comedy is lacking.

THEME STATEMENT

In one sense Theodora was the better for the purging by fire. No longer asking why God does this or that, she decides to renew her search by returning to the black hills of Australia. She goes by way of America. Traveling west across the continent by train she sees, in her day-to-day solitude, the endless corn and waving hills. She learns what Voss and Laura came to understand. She says to herself, "There is sometimes little to choose between the reality of illusion and the illusion of reality."

Her capacity for clear thinking gradually worsens. In a moment either of panic or transcendental perception, she leaves the train at a way station.

CLEANSING WATER AND CLEANSING FIRE

Having wandered away from the train stop and civilization into almost barren countryside, she is befriended by the Johnsons, a happy family with children. When Mrs. Johnson brings water to Theo to wash with, we are reminded both of the New Testament (the story of Martha and Mary) and the Odyssey. As the nurse recognized the traveler Odysseus through all his grime, so Mrs. Johnson recognizes the truth about Theodora. She is mad. Along with the fact that water cannot wash away madness, White seems to offer the suggestion that madness itself may be a cleanser. However, before the Johnsons arrange for her to be put away, another symbol is introduced. Theo stumbles upon the hut of the hermit, Holstius ("an almost anagram of holiest"). As she is building a fire, she rocks on her heels when Holstius appears on the other side of the flames. Here we are reminded of the prophet Ezekiel. Repeating his use of fire as a universal cleanser, White has Holstius bring peace to Theodora. She learns from him in moments of lucidity that joy and sorrow are permanent parts of life and also death. Thereby she gains strength. After Holstius has gone she rolls up her sleeves and scrubs the floor in a scene similar to that repeated by Mary de Santis in *The Eye of the Storm*. Through the foaming suds she washes her sins away. Theodora is triumphant. She is still feeling her victory when a doctor comes to take her away. Mrs. Johnson brings Theodora Goodman her hat. God is her umbrella. "The hat sat straight, but the doubtful rose trembled and glittered, leading a life of its own."

THE TREE OF MAN

AUTHOR'S PURPOSE

When White returned from England where he had written *The Aunt's Story*, he wanted, as an Australian, to write an all-Australian novel. At the same time he wanted it to be free of the journalistic realism of his immediate Australian predecessors and contemporaries. His self-admitted desire was to portray ordinary people with almost biblical simplicity as they were at the time when Sydney was beginning to expand into what would become its suburbs. A certain amount of condescension might be expected from an author deliberately writing about ordinary people, but White characteristically shows how much the ordinary are capable of the extraordinary.

From White's choice of names for his characters we are immediately forewarned of the story's action. Stanley Parker is certainly steadfast and upright. He parks on the land he, without help, hews and chops out of the bush. Amy, his wife who also parked there, is romantic and creates the tension implied by her significant name (Amy - amo, amas, amat, etc.).

THE MYSTERY AND THE POETRY

This is not merely a novel about a place but a place that becomes a home. From the moment Amy plants a white rose bush in front of what was still little more than a shack, we are aware of her yearning intent. Whatever their challenges and their disappointments, the Parkers are always compensated by the peacefulness of Stan's greening fields. Nevertheless, Amy is restless, especially in the long years before she has a child of her own. She has a high degree of self-interest. She is less concerned by the countryside than by what it can produce. She has a desire for possessions which makes us recognize her as a forerunner of White's young Elizabeth Hunter of *The Eye of the Storm*.

HUMAN COMMUNICATION

Regardless of their love, Amy and Stan often fail to communicate. In particular, this turns Stan into a lonely person such as no novel of White's is without. Similarly, this is true of his wife who surprises herself with an infidelity with a total stranger. The novel unfolds as an engrossing study of human relationships. Stan withdraws more into himself, more so after his return from World War I, which plays little part in the novel, except as his absence affects his home about which he is less materially mindful. They talk less and less together. Their children, instead of bringing the parents together, become reflections of what is most wrong with each. Personal tensions are released without violence although the novel contains considerable violent drama. There are two big fire episodes. These are externals made subordinate to the internal conflagrations the characters undergo. However, these two are never completely purged. It is their suspension that makes many consider the book a tragedy.

IDIOM OF THE NOVEL

The Parkers' lack of verbal ability is a characteristic we can perceive in the novel's dialogue. There is a certain thickness of expression which demonstrates White's capacity to achieve perfect coincidence of words, thoughts, and feelings. The ordinariness of the Parker language is so decently simple that their extraordinary, even poetic, sensitivity gradually forces the reader to admire them. They are no fools. Both are intelligent and knowledgeable and both are enhanced by the permanency of their position. White makes this clear when the Parkers are contrasted, first with the affluent Sydneysiders gradually forsaking their town for suburbia, and secondly with their first neighbors, the slovenly O'Dowds. The high comedy scene when the drunken O'Dowd chases his wife and Amy about their crazy house with a shotgun is one of the earliest but one of the best of White's set pieces. Its roughness may lack the sardonic and vicious **satire** of the author's later **episodes** but it is every bit as hilariously funny.

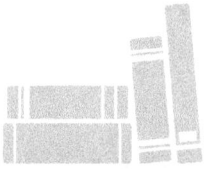

RIDERS IN THE CHARIOT

THE TRAVELERS

This is the first of the novels to appear after the fame brought by *Voss*. It is noteworthy because its symbolism actually carries the story. The Christ figure is dominant but, as in all of White's identifications, the symbol varies from tradition. First of all the symbol is multiplied. There are four characters, all in some way saviors. They support White's propensity for the quaternary structure. Since they are all riders in the fiery chariot of Ezekiel and also of Apollo, they demonstrate White's bent for mixing Hebraic and Greek tradition. The theory that all myths were born of a common origin is accordingly supported.

WHO'S WHO

Once again names are important. Each character has a name related in some way to a visionary ideal. They foreshadow the tension created by each coming in contact with the other. What each has in common with the other and what each recognizes in the others confirm White's ability to show that Christ-like characteristics are not confined to any inherited or acquired time or place.

The first of the four is Mary Hare. Her name is twice meaningful. Mary is a virgin and also a hare, an animal usually painted by medieval artists at the Holy Mother's feet to indicate her triumph over physical nature. Mary Hare is usually humble with humans, some of whom she recognizes with a sort of sixth sense as being marked with the sign of Cain. Sometimes she is a mad hare.

Next there is Mordecai Himmelfarb whose first name identifies him with death (mort) and whose surname roughly translated means blue heaven. At the Australian airport the pillar of fire that precedes him may be linked to a similar one that preceded his forefathers on their journey to the Promised Land. He is the subject of a cruel joke which kills him on Good Friday. By then he is undeniably a Christ figure.

The second woman is Ruth Godbold. She is faithful to her responsibilities to the end and thereby suggests the biblical Ruth.

The black man is the fourth rider, Dubbo. His name may have exotic aboriginal meaning to some readers. Yet knowing White, we may guess a multilinguistic connection to the French du beau, from or of the good. It is a mark of White's genius to lift them out of the Australian township of Sarsaparilla (his own Yoknapawtpha) and to put the four of them in the same chariot. He links them together by their guilts. White's sense of guilt differs, as might be expected, from usual Western tradition, though some may say he brings Hawthorne and Melville up to date. The guilt differs because in each case each character thinks he committed a sin. Theirs were transgressions in thought rather than in deed. With White the ambivalence of guilt is the determinant of character and action. Mary Hare thinks she murdered her father (whom she hated) when she perhaps had the power to save him after he fell down a well. (His suicide is not ruled out.) Himmelfarb thinks of himself as a coward who might have been able to save his wife when the Nazis set their house afire. Ruth believes her carelessness when minding her small brother cost him his life. Dubbo never forgives himself for running away from the white brother and sister who loved and protected him. He does not die until he, like Peter, has betrayed the "crucified" Himmelfarb.

The novel is also typically White in its many symbols - the plum tree, the chain, the rope, the ladder, the stick, the veils, and many more. There are comic set pieces including one in a transvestite setting. There are representatives of an emerging Australian life style more often treated with sarcasm than kindliness. Among these we have Mr. Rosetree, an apostate born Rosenbaum, Mrs. Jolley whose name fails to mask her cruelty, and Mrs. Flack, the meaning of whose name is obvious.

MEANING OF FICTION

A parallelism has been pointed out between this novel and S. T. Coleridge's "Kubla Khan." This is suggested by Zanadu, Mary Hare's home, under which runs a subterranean river that surfaces momentarily as another did under Xanadu. The meaning of Coleridge's poem has long been disputed. Since "Kubla Khan" is not entirely emotional but logically precise, the concept that its meaning is the meaning of all poetry has been maintained. In the same sense, it has been asserted the meaning of White's novel is a credo of a novelist on novels. Because the precise structure of *The Riders in the Chariot* defies poetic analysis, this idea gains support.

THE SOLID MANDALA

ONE PLUS ONE

This novel, first published in 1966, has been called the author's "warmest" perhaps because of the character of Arthur who loves and is loved. However, Arthur is only one of twin brothers. The other is Waldo who hates.

The **theme** is of the same lineage as the earlier books, yet in White fashion it is full of surprises. There is a great deal of submerged symbolism and it is wise to remember Oscar Wilde's comment, "Those who read the symbol do so at their own peril." Because White offers his readers so many clues, the risk is diminished.

The central symbol is the mandala, which like a boy's marble, is a sphere or universe. A symbol of unity, it is used in Yoga as an aid to contemplation. Its oneness is unifying. White uses it to suggest a synthesis of all the world's great mythologies and religions. It promotes his **theme** that love and humility are twin necessities and the corollary that reason is often inadequate.

The twin brothers are two. Two squared is four. At the outset the boys' parents are alive. Later two female characters make up the foursome: Dulcie, the healthy and earthbound young woman who attracts both brothers, and Mrs. Poulter, the boys' neighbor and mother surrogate. The quaternary system is manipulated with White's customary skill. The novel is divided into four unequal parts. The first and last may be called Mrs. Poulter's. Her way of life and speech are most typical of Australian suburbia. She rides the bus (the journey motif) from the town Sarsaparilla, to Barranugli (bare and ugly). The two central sections are variations on the same story, the one from Waldo's viewpoint, the other Arthur's corrections. Waldo is a pseudo-intellectual and works in the library. In him White is acidic on the subject of Australian literature and its pretensions. With Arthur, an alleged "dill" who works as a grocery clerk, White is proclaiming to his peers that the most ordinary Australian can be viewed as a fascinating human being.

Waldo sees himself as the leader and protector of his simple brother. Arthur, who indeed feels protected, is in truth the protector. White is exploring the twin parts of man, how flesh and spirit are dependent on each other. The twin, a result of fission, becomes a symbol of fusion, a mandala.

The boy Arthur has four marbles. One he gives to Dulcie as a love symbol; one to Mrs. Poulter whose child (even though a grown man) he becomes; one is rejected by his brother and is lost; one he keeps, signifying his own integrity.

Besides the overtones that suggest the story of Cain and Abel, The Brothers Karamazov, Yeats' Mask concept, and Plato's parable of two yolks in one shell, the story is not lacking in action, sometimes violent, or in romance which is more sympathetic than usually found in White. Also there are several funny scenes during the seventy years the twins live together.

THE VIVISECTOR

TRAGIC DILEMMA

Published in 1970, *The Vivisector* received the highest praise of any novel White had written up to that date. It surely played a part in the 1973 decision of the Nobel Prize Committee. The entire spectrum of Australian society from the turn of the century forward is brilliantly encircled about the violent, passionate, mentally furious life of its central figure, the painter, Hurtle Duffield. (Hurtle, hurtling, Du du, of the field, of the earth.)

Because this novel is a portrait of an artist, James Joyce's *A Portrait of the Artist as a Young Man* invites comparison. Also several passages suggest Joycean epiphanies. However, it was not Joyce who was chosen for comparison by Patricia A. Morley in her review in the *Queen's Quarterly*, Autumn, 1971, Kingston, Ontario. In her essay called "The Doppelganger's Dilemma; Artist and Man," she wrote: "Rimbaud's life and works show close parallels to motives and characters in White's latest novel. White sympathizes with Rimbaud's romantic view of the artist. His protagonist, Hurtle Duffield, experiences the potentially tragic dilemma of being both artist and man. White's triumphant solution of the problem is part of the novel's success."

EXTRA DIMENSIONS

Duffield puts to the service of his art all life, high and low. Even partial truth can be visualized only through discipline. Duffield, who, as a small boy, was sold by his laundress mother for more money than she had ever seen before, tries continuously to escape from the fearful isolation that inevitably followed. As another artist, Delacroix said, "Loneliness is the torment of my soul."

As a man Duffield seeks nourishment through close association with other human beings. We are intrigued by White's insight into the many minor characters of the book. Sex and its extension into love play a more open and important part than in his earlier novels. White uses four women to reveal the character of his artist **protagonist**. Each views and touches him from a different angle. Each paints part of the portrait. This gives us the feeling of walking around a piece of sculpture. First there is Olivia, a childhood friend of his sister. Later after her marriage to a very wealthy man, this masculine type of woman becomes one of the most devoted promoters of his artistic reputation. Then, there is Nance Bloody, the unsentimentalized prostitute. She is White's version of the bad woman with a lot of good in her. Her trade is her art: "Because I do it good." Next is the adolescent Kathy who seduces the middle-aged painter. He needs her as a source of extra creative strength. Herself an artist, she becomes a piano virtuoso of worldwide fame. Last, there is Hero Pavloussis, the wife of a Greek tycoon whom she deserts for Duffield. Their lust is violent to the point of obscenity. Both pass through psychic hell for each other. Paradoxically, their union becomes his atonement.

> **DIG IN**

There is still another woman who weaves in and out of the story. She is the crippled daughter of the wealthy couple who bought and legally adopted Hurtle. The **theme** of divine cruelty is expressed in her deformity. Her almost superhuman struggle to come to terms with a loving God is at the root of the artist's own. To him, for most of his life, God is the vivisector. Why do we have incurables? Later, and very gradually, God is conceived as an artist, the artist, the first creator. Then finally, God.

The destruction of the vivisector is the novel's central **theme**. It is highlighted at the end by one of White's typical word plays. He concentrates on I-N-D-I-G-O. (As might be expected in a book about a painter, the dominant symbols are colors.) From this word many others may be formed - DIG - DOG - DOING, but finally there emerges "I GO" - to sleep forever, NOD.

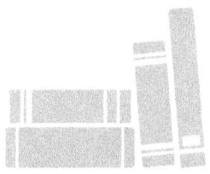

QUESTIONS AND ANSWERS IN OUTLINE FORM

....

1. What is the dominant **theme** of *The Eye of the Storm*?

Answer. Depending on the reader the choice may vary, but consideration should be given to the following:

    a. **A human being can obtain complete peace within himself.**

    b. **Only a thin line separates illusion from reality.**

    c. **No human being is free from loneliness.**

    d. **Sentiment should not interfere with the search for truth.**

2. How does evil bring out the good in Elizabeth Hunter?

Answer. Here the following points may be included:

    a. **Vanity seen in others makes her resist her own.**

    b. **Greed makes her generous.**

    c. **Stupidity makes her cautious.**

    d. **Lust makes her recognize love.**

3. What is the role of the Australian aborigine in *Voss*?

Answer. Included should be the facts that aborigines:

    a. **Serve as an anchorage to an Australia that is not English.**

    b. **Serve as figures that demand tolerance for all minorities.**

    c. **Serve as pathways to unsophisticated truths.**

    d. **Serve as artistic inspiration.**

4. What are the major characteristics of White's style?

Answer. Include here:

    a. **Lucidity resulting from precise use of words and word sequences.**

    b. **Ability to use language as varied by social class and individual psychology.**

    c. **Ability to compress thought by the use of poetic figures of speech.**

    d. **Rhythmic cadences that vary with mood.**

    e. **Willingness to experiment with words and grammar.**

5. How does White use symbols as signals?

Answer. Not to be omitted are:

    a. **Soap and water to signal cleansing.**

    b. **Hairiness to signal a sex episode.**

    c. **Blueness to signal purity.**

    d. **Hats to signal protection.**

6. Of what significance are White's set comic pieces?

Answer. Any one of the following may be developed:

    a. **They serve to heighten drama.**

    b. **They serve as transitions from the individual to the universal.**

    c. **They serve as gadflies that sting one into seeing what is unacceptable in oneself.**

    d. **They are enjoyably funny.**

7. In what ways are White's chief characters linked from novel to novel?

Answer. Here it should be stressed that all central figures are:

    a. **Visionaries.**

    b. **Alienated.**

    c. **Willful.**

    d. **Productive.**

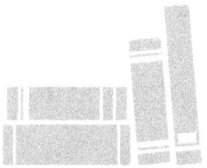

BIBLIOGRAPHY

PATRICK WHITE - NOVELS

Happy Valley. London 1939, 1940. New York 1940.

The Living and the Dead. Toronto 1941. London 1941, 1962. New York 1941.

The Aunt's Story. Toronto 1948. London 1948, 1958. New York 1949, 1962. Melbourne 1963.

The Tree of Man. Toronto 1955. New York 1955. London 1956.

Voss. London 1957, 1958, 1959, 1962, 1965. New York 1957.

Riders in the Chariot. London 1961. New York 1961.

The Solid Mandala. London 1966. New York 1966.

The Vivisector. London 1970. New York 1970.

The Eye of the Storm. London 1973. New York 1973.

CRITICISM IN PERIODICALS

For book reviews and articles about Patrick White the student is referred to"

Reader's Guide to Periodical Literature

Book Review Index

Times Literary Supplement, London. Sept. 21, 1973 (for special review of *The Eye of the Storm* entitled "High Wind in Australia")

For Australian and New Zealand criticism:

Beston, John B. "Alienation and Humanization: Damnation and Salvation in *Voss*," *Meanjin* (Victoria), XXX:2, June, 1971.

Edmund, Murray. "Entering the Eye," *Cave* (Dunedin, N.Z.), III and IV, February and November, 1973.

Mather, Rodney. "Patrick White and Lawrence: A Contrast," *Critical Review* (Melbourne), XIII, 1970.

Smith, Terry. "A Portrait of the Artist in Patrick White's *The Vivisector*," *Meanjin* (Victoria), XXXI:2, June 1970.

Watson, Betty L. "Patrick White: Some Lines of Development: The Living and the Dead to *The Solid Mandala*," *Australian Literary Studies* (University of Tasmania), V:2, October 1971. (Same number contains article by John B. Beston on Patrick White.)

For Canadian criticism:

Beston, Rose Marie. The **Theme** of Spiritual Progression in *Voss*," *Ariel* (Calgary), V:3, July, 1974.

CRITICISM AND BACKGROUND MATERIAL IN BOOKS

Argyle, Barry. *Patrick White*. Edinburgh and London: Oliver and Boyd, 1967.

Beebe, Maurice (Editor). *Literary Symbolism*: *An Anthology*. San Francisco: Wadsworth Publishing Co., 1960.

Brissenden, R. F. *Patrick White in* "Writers and Their Work" Series; #190. London: Longmans, Green & Co. Ltd., 1966.

Brooks, Cleanth. *A Shaping Joy: Studies in The Writer's Craft*. London: Methuen & Co. Ltd., 1973.

Buckley, V. "The Novels of Patrick White" in *The Literature of Australia*, ed. G. Dutton, Melbourne: Oxford University Press, 1964.

Cranstone, B. A. L. *The Australian Aborigines*. London: The British Museum, 1973.

Dutton, Geoffrey. *Patrick White*. Melbourne: Oxford University Press, 1961, Revised 1971.

Gunther, John. *Inside Australia* (completed and edited by W. H. Forbis). New York: Harper & Row, 1972.

Johnston, George. *My Brother Jack*. London and Sydney: Collins, 1964. (An outstanding Australian novel.)

Maddock, Kenneth. *The Australian Aborigines: A Portrait of Their Society*. London: Allen Lane, 1973.

Morley, Patricia A. *The Mystery of Unity: Theme and Technique in the Novels of Patrick White*. Montreal and London*:* McGill-Queens University Press, 1972.

Turner, G. W. *The English Language in Australia and New Zealand.* London: Longmans, 1966.

Walsh, William. *Commonwealth Literature.* London: Oxford University Press, 1973.

Weston, Jessie L. *From Ritual to Romance.* New York: Doubleday Anchor Book, 1957.

Wilkes, G. A. *Australian Literature - A Conspectus.* London: Angus and Robertson Ltd., 1970.